Creating Literacy-Rich Preschools and Kindergartens

D0128481

Creating Literacy-Rich Preschools and Kindergartens

Anne K. Soderman
Michigan State University

Patricia Farrell
Michigan State University

Boston   New York   San Francisco
Mexico City   Montreal   Toronto   London   Madrid   Munich   Paris
Hong Kong   Singapore   Tokyo   Cape Town   Sydney

Executive Editor: *Aurora Martínez Ramos*
Editorial Assistant: *Lynda Giles*
Marketing Manager: *Danae April*
Production Editor: *Janet Domingo*
Editorial Production Service: *Publishers' Design and Production Services, Inc.*
Composition Buyer: *Linda Cox*
Manufacturing Buyer: *Linda Morris*
Electronic Composition: *Publishers' Design and Production Services, Inc.*
Cover Administrator: *Joel Gendron*

For related titles and support materials, visit our online catalog at www.ablongman.com.

Copyright © 2008 Pearson Education, Inc.

All rights reserved. No part of the material protected by this copyright notice may be reproduced or utilized in any form or by any means, electronic or mechanical, including photocopying, recording, or by any information storage and retrieval system, without written permission from the copyright owner.

To obtain permission(s) to use material from this work, please submit a written request to Allyn and Bacon, Permissions Department, 75 Arlington Street, Boston, MA 02116, or fax your request to 617-848-7320.

Between the time Website information is gathered and then published, it is not unusual for some sites to have closed. Also, the transcription of URLs can result in unintended typographical errors. The publisher would appreciate notification where these errors occur so that they may be corrected in subsequent editions.

ISBN 10: 0-205-45573-5
ISBN 13: 978-0-205-45573-7

Library of Congress Cataloging-in-Publication Data
Soderman, Anne Keil.
    Creating literacy-rich preschools and kindergartens / Anne K. Soderman, Patricia Farrell.
        p. cm.
    Includes bibliographical references and index.
    ISBN 0-205-45573-5 (alk. paper)
    1. Language arts (Preschool)—United States. 2. Language arts (Kindergarten)—United States. 3. Literacy—United States. I. Farrell, Patricia. II. Title.
    LB1140.5.L3S63 2008
    372.6—dc22   2006036758

Printed in the United States of America

10 9 8 7 6 5 4 3 2 1   11 10 09 08 07

Photo credits: Page 1, Corbis; page 20, Image 100; page 53, Photodisc/Getty Images; page 98, Bill Burlingham/Prentice Hall School Division; page 121, iStock.

Contents

CHAPTER 3

Emerging Literacy Components and Teaching Strategies 53

CHAPTER 4

The Child's World outside the Classroom: Involving Families as Partners in the Literacy Process 98

CHAPTER 5

Useful and Authentic Assessment
Strategies   121

Preface

The catalyst for this book came out of a project on which we collaborated over a multiyear period with urban kindergarten and Michigan School Readiness Program, Head Start teachers. Both children and professionals seemed to be struggling with building strong early literacy skills, concepts, and practices. We wondered whether we could make a difference in the literacy skill levels of children who had been identified as likely to have significant learning difficulties in the early grades. These were children who already had noticeable deficiencies in vocabulary, literacy experiences and concepts, and social interaction—and they weren't even first graders yet!

As we began to work with the teachers, administrators, school staff, and parents involved, we first applied a number of strategies and ideas we had used in more than two decades of what we believed was effective teacher training. However, as we learned more about the needs of the teachers, we knew we were going to have to add to our own repertoire and expand our expectations of how they would implement daily literacy interactions with children. Simply offering workshops on best practice didn't result in the change in practice we had hoped for. That took structuring a more collaborative staff development process that involved site observation, discussion to promote understanding, greater sharing of ideas, and firmer commitment on the part of the adults to bring research-based practice into the children's everyday experiences.

We also learned more about our own assumptions related to how parents can work as true partners in fostering learning in the early years. We came away from the project concluding that children from high-risk populations—indeed, all children—can make significant gains in emerging literacy skills and concepts during the early years, but only if adults carefully and responsibly structure the literacy environment. In other words, it cannot be business as usual. With the cooperation of the teachers and parents, we were able to implement consistent, high-quality best practices and rigorous evaluation of children's growth, optimizing each child's chance to be a more successful learner. We believe these ideas will work well in all early literacy contexts where professionals are hoping to build children's emerging oral language skills, alphabetic knowledge, phonological awareness, and concepts of print.

Acknowledgment

We would like to thank the W. K. Kellogg Foundation for its generous support of the Capital Area Youth Alliance (CAYA) Transition to Kindergarten project that led to the development of this text. We owe much to Erin Groom, photographer, for her expertise and ability to capture the essence of high quality early childhood settings and children's reactions to good teaching. We would also like to recognize the support and cooperation of the following partners in this project: Lansing-area public schools; Capital Area Community Services Head Start director Lucy McClintic and Head Start teachers; the teachers and administrators at Cornerstone School in Ocala, Florida; Michigan State University graduate students Erica Poindexter and Toko Oshio; Lynne Martinez in her role as executive director of CAYA. We appreciate the parents who enrolled their children in the summer programs, made sure they got there each day, and extended literacy activities in the home. We would also like to thank Felicia Hobbs, Dr. Patricia H. Kostell, Martha Navarro, and Teresa Richardson for their thoughtful comments and review of the manuscript. We are grateful to the staff at Allyn & Bacon, particularly Aurora Martínez and her extremely competent assistant Lynda Giles, for getting these ideas to print.

We are especially appreciative to the preschool and kindergarten teachers in the Lansing school district who taught in the summer programs, participated in carrying out the suggested activities, and allowed us to observe their practice and photograph their classrooms. Their cooperation, suggestions, and insights were invaluable in completing this work. Finally, we express our appreciation to the children in these programs who provided work samples and thumbs-up or thumbs-down responses to indicate which of the activities were the most meaningful, useful, and engaging as they moved toward greater understanding of the power and wonder of print.

Anne K. Soderman
Patricia Farrell

Creating Literacy-Rich Preschools and Kindergartens

Chapter 1

Introduction

Early childhood education is, indeed, a hot item today, and most of the heat has centered on **emerging literacy.** How young children become literate is receiving a great deal of attention today—in local school districts, in Washington, DC, and across the nation. Characteristics of emerging readers, learning contexts, teaching strategies, the role of parents in supporting emerging literacy in their children, and **assessment** practices are all under the microscope. The purpose of this publication is to summarize current knowledge and best practices about each of these components to get our youngest learners, particularly those who come from tough situations, off to the best possible start.

"Early childhood development and early childhood education are hot items these days. Brain research, Head Start, early education opportunities, early intervention, and many other issues related to funding, policies, facilities, and curriculum for young children seem omnipresent in both professional and public media."

WILLIAM H. TEALE

If you are a preschool or kindergarten teacher, or an administrator in a context that houses an early childhood education program, you have no doubt felt a little of this heat. We hope you will find the information gathered in each chapter useful, meaningful, and engaging, and that you will be able to apply the ideas effectively in your work with young learners and their families.

Transformations in Early Childhood Education: Are We on the Right Path?

We are still very much in a learning mode about the best match between the young child's developmental needs and changing demands in early learning environments. There is little doubt that a significant transformation has taken place in early childhood education. The traditional play-based preschool and kindergarten programs that focused so heavily on social–emotional development have been replaced with a heavy emphasis on literacy and numeracy.

Despite these obvious and relatively abrupt changes, attention to developmentally appropriate practice hangs on. Knowledgeable early childhood professionals have found a way to tie together children's dif-

fering developmental levels with expectations and desired curricular outcomes that are also critical to a young child's overall development. These teachers have been creative in folding literacy learning tasks into children's play and integrating other domains. They have always been expert in using a mixture of individual, small-group, and large-group venues for instruction, and center-based strategies from early childhood education have now found their way into many elementary and middle school classrooms. One of the greatest changes in preschool and kindergarten education has been in the area of assessment. Significantly more attention is being given to developing authentic informal assessment strategies to measure progress, sometimes to ward off the use of inappropriate practices and tools.

Teacher inservice has been intensive during the past decade, and attendance at such conferences as the International Reading Association (IRA), Association for Childhood Education International (ACEI), Association for Supervision and Curriculum Development (ASCD), Society for Research on Child Development (SRCD), and National Association for the Education of Young Children (NAEYC) have been popular with early educators in a hurry to learn more about young children and research-based practice. Professional organizations such as the IRA and NAEYC have written joint statements about standards for learning and appropriate ways to measure children's progress. We've come a long way, but according to Teale (2003, 29–33), there are still a number of questions that need clearer answers. The following are six questions he poses and our responses to those queries:

*What kinds of classroom **oral language** activities contribute significantly to early literacy learning?* To answer this, we are going to have to pay greater attention to documenting systematically the kinds and quality of vocabulary instructional experiences to which our youngest children are exposed. Moreover, we need to study the effects longitudinally.

It is our thesis that, currently, there isn't *enough* emphasis on oral language in almost any of our early childhood settings; rather, schedules are filled almost completely with **phonemic awareness,** prereading, and prewriting activities. This is not to say that we don't give plenty of lip service to the importance of oral language as a critical foundation for later reading skill. We just don't see much instructional planning and implementation in this area. Nor do we see enough prompts in the commercial curricular materials that are produced. It's as if we believe that as long as children are engaged in conversation with others, enrichment in vocabulary and more sophisticated semantic and syntactic language development will emerge naturally. As we're finding out, this isn't necessarily true, and a part of every day's instruction should include active attention to vocabulary and language enhancement. In Chapter 3, we suggest a number of oral language activities and hope you plan your day so that there is a balance in the literacy activities you offer. In addition, we are hopeful that school systems and university researchers will begin to track statistically the correlations that can be found between children's early experiences and later literacy outcomes.

How much do independent reading activities help children become capable, comprehending readers—and what kinds of activities are helpful? Teale's interest here clearly lies in the debate about whether it's useful to take instructional time to have children engaging in sustained silent reading. Pat Cunningham (2005) notes that rather than using the 15 minutes a day to model her own interest in reading to the children, she would insert individual conferences once a week during that time to talk with each child (dividing the class into five different groups and putting a struggling reader in each group). Being sure to make the conference more like a conversation than an "interrogation," she and the child would have time to talk about the content of the child's reading choice. She could then monitor what the child is getting out of the experience and provide needed encouragement through undivided attention.

Not everything that happens in a classroom needs to be—or should be—directed teaching. Practice, which children need to cement concepts and skills, is often relegated to homework. Too often, in a good part of the population, homework often doesn't happen—or doesn't happen very well. We must be patient enough to "give up" some of our direct instructional time to allow for complementary practice time. In addition, we talk about enjoyment of reading as one of our goals for children. If this is to be more than just rhetoric, time should be allocated in a child's primary learning context for it to happen. We need to examine how well we structure the environment to entice independent literacy activity. And if teachers *do* include time for children to participate in cozy reading corners and nooks and interesting writing centers, is there a connection to later reading skill and interest? What do we know about offering different literacy **genres** to children and later literacy behaviors? What happens when lap reading is missing in a child's preschool years and is not offered in the early childhood classroom? How knowledgeable are teachers about scaffolding early reading and

writing experiences so that children can become increasingly independent in using print? How are early drawing and writing connected to the child's later storytelling and comprehension skills? Does consistent, daily journal writing in the preschool and kindergarten classroom really count in the long run? Answers to these questions can only come when educators begin to connect the dots between what happens within and between educational contexts, looking over a number of years and at the same children. Good ethnographic research must also get at the differing gender, chronological, experiential, language, and ethnic/cultural differences that confound so many of our studies, in addition to the movement of children from teacher to teacher in the preprimary and primary grades.

What role should phonemic awareness instruction play in the reading/language arts curriculum? In our estimation, the controversy about whether **phonics** and phonemic awareness instruction should be included in preschool and kindergarten is overblown. We do it when we play Silly Names with children, exchanging the initial consonant in their names with others. We do it when we show them the magic of **onsets and rimes.** *How* this instruction is provided is our concern. It is only when we see kindergarten children being *timed* on their ability to identify phonemes that we want to step in. It is when phonemic awareness instruction becomes *laborious* for children in early childhood settings or when it dominates the curriculum that we become concerned. It is when worksheets and drill overtake more meaningful activity that can teach letter–sound and letter–grapheme associations that we know we've gone too far!

Teaching children **letter–sound association** is necessary, and we no longer believe that the best way to have children develop phonemic awareness is to let them simply bump into it. The alphabet, and all the wonderful things human beings have been able to do in manipulating it, is not built into the human species, as is rudimentary language and speech. The **alphabetic principle** and phonemic awareness are part of the conventional knowledge that children must learn to read and write well, and we are hopeful that many of the developmentally appropriate activities presented in this text will not only promote phonemic awareness among the children in your classroom, but delight them as well.

Conversely, when early childhood classrooms become so overly focused on phonemic awareness instruction that children begin to think of reading as decoding a series of sounds, it's time to take a step back. Scharer, Pinnell, Lyons, and Fountas (2005, 25) warn against overloading beginning readers with forced and scripted reading programs, basal readers and workbooks in place of children's literature, and giving up on developmentally appropriate activities in favor of teaching phonics out of context. Reading, they say, "is thinking cued by written language," and they want children to know that, too. Effective readers will have participated in numerous activities that teach them to think within the text, beyond the text, and about the text.

Which types of texts help beginning readers learn to read—and what ways do they help? Having grown up reading the very predictable Dick and Jane series, we remember not being absolutely thrilled about the exploits of Puff, Baby, Jane, and whoever the dog was. But we do remember being thrilled that because of the safety of the controlled vocabulary and high decodability, we were actually reading very quickly! Of course, that was not all we read. There were also books of

rhyme, fairy tales, and comic books to decipher. We loved listening to the teacher and our mother (sorry, Dad) read all kinds of books, some of which supplied us with the more complex vocabulary, story elements, and sentence patterns that would drive us to be readers, then and now.

Estimates are that at least one in five U.S. children with average or above average intelligence has trouble associating speech sounds with corresponding letters and learning to read (Bower, 2004). Perhaps what we need to study is how and what happens when children get stuck, for one reason or another, in lower level reading achievement. Does it have more to do with using highly decodable text or more to do with not offering *more* than decodable text at the same time? What role does the competition from technology play today in children choosing *not* to read in their leisure time? How much of failure is truly biological in nature? Have we gone far enough in documenting gender and ethnic differences, and how many of the differences eventually disappear?

What types of instruction programs best meet the needs of children of color and children from low-income backgrounds? Alfie Kohn (2004) has written that the thing standardized tests tell us best of all is the *address* of the test taker. The dearth of literacy experiences and models for children coming from low-income backgrounds may create the differences that have been clearly documented. In terms of the ethnic differences that persist (although the gap is narrowing), they may not be so much a result of ethnicity as a result of poverty, second language difficulties, perspectives about bleak futures, and related motivations to learn that dominate certain ethnic groups. Our tendency to draw conclusions from general statistical findings among ethnic groups without controlling for income, family status, parent education, and other confounding factors may lead us to believe that children of color and those who come from low-income populations are different than other children in their potential to learn or *ways in which* they enjoy learning.

Although the debate about the value of developmentally appropriate practice (DAP) versus more didactic approaches in early childhood continues, we see evidence that there is a struggle to regain some of what has been lost. In considering diversity, Kostelnik, Soderman, and Whiren (2007) have gathered evidence that positive program results associated with DAP are evident for boys and for girls, for children from higher income families and lower income families, and for European American, Native American, and African American youngsters. These results seem to support the idea that children benefit from DAP even when their backgrounds are diverse. Conversely, substantial inequities exist for children in classrooms categorized as developmentally *inappropriate*. In such programs, girls, children of higher socioeconomic status, and white children all perform better and report less stressful experiences than do boys, children of lower socioeconomic status, Native American children, and African American children (Charlesworth, Hart, Burts, Thomasson, Mosely, & Fleege, 1993; Dunn & Kontos, 1997; Hart, Burts, Durland, Charlesworth, DeWolf, & Fleege, 1998; Little-Soldier, 1992; Soderman, Gregory, McCarty, 2005). The whole concept of DAP is that we are committed to try as hard as we can to meet the needs of individual children, even if it means that we must lean toward more didactic practices for some children. If we are to give each child in our classrooms what he or she needs, there is only one thing that is certain: We cannot have every child on page 57 of the workbook, deliver instruction in exactly the same way, or expect a child to pick up a concept or skill as quickly as another child might.

What classroom literacy assessment instruments can be made available to teachers so that they can obtain diagnostic infor-

mation about individual students that enables effective literacy instruction? We believe that evaluation and confirmation of growth are so important that we have devoted an entire chapter (Chapter 5) in this text to assessment. Although we have suggested several standardized instruments that might be more diagnostic in nature, we feel these usually only document what experienced teachers already know—that a child is behind his or her peers in learning or applying learning. It is the informal, performance-based samples of the child's work on a day-to-day basis that will provide what teachers need to know to scaffold the child as rigorously as possible toward the next level of success. This said, when children go too far afield from their peer group in any developmental domain and are at a standstill despite our best strategies to address the differences, we need to call in a relevant specialist for another opinion and possible intervention.

Young Children as Emerging Literacy Learners

How human beings learn anything, including the abilities necessary to read and write, has become somewhat clearer during the past five years, as brain imaging technology and solid research have developed. Some of the mysteries of cognitive and early literacy development are now being unlocked by neuroscientists who study the developing brain and its ability to identify, attend to, and act on complex stimuli. Using imaging techniques such as positron emission technology scans and functional magnetic resonance imaging, brain scientists have provided us with information about children's developing memory, ability to concentrate, reasoning, and emotional behavior (Restak, 2003).

Two processes are involved in early brain development that are relevant for us to think about: synapse development (cognitive arborization) and pruning. Even before birth and afterward, there are periods of rapid synaptogenesis, or connections being made within many of approximately 100 billion neurons. The density that develops from all these connections results in an inefficient brain and, at approximately 18 months, the process of pruning begins in the human organism and continues throughout life. Needed connections are constructed and strengthened through reinforcement and use; conversely, unused synaptic connections are eventually discarded. Although we don't have

Lindsey

My favorite show is Power Puff Girls. My favorite restaurant is Flap Jack. My favorite colors are silver and gold. I like to play with Nicole. I like pancakes. I like to watch Channel 38.

Matt

My favorite food is hamburgers. My favorite cartoon Dexter's Laboratory. I like to watch Channel 60. I like to eat at Red Lobster. My favorite pants are my tiger pants.

Erika

My favorite color is blue. I like tacos. My favorite show is Power Puff girls. I like to color flowers. MY favorite place is the Disney Store. My favorite restaurant is Red Lobster.

any evidence that making environments or experiences more complex will *increase* neural synapse material in human beings, research documents that stimulation maintains connections, and that deprived environments in childhood lack of sufficient nutrition, health care, and/or auditory stimulation are associated with greater neural pruning (Gallagher, 2005, 12–13). Apparently, effects of the environment on brain development are maximal between late infancy and late childhood. This is a period when enrichment is likely to have the greatest effect (Huttenlocher, 2002).

We also know that there's a difference in how quickly and efficiently human beings can access information when they've had a lot of experience and practice with something. Thus, children who have been exposed to different kinds and amounts of print from birth are able to recognize patterns and to associate sounds with abstract symbols related to print much more easily than those who lack such exposure.

If human beings are motivated to want to stretch themselves to become better at something, they are more likely to achieve higher performance levels (Ericsson, 2002). In children, the mental schemes (or scripts or frames) that they develop are intimately connected to their developing attitudes, values, and aims. These frames "function as selective mechanisms that influence the information individuals attend to, how they structure it, how much importance they attach to it, and what they then do with it" (VanderZanden, 2003, 49). Translating this to developing literacy, and remembering that emerging literacy is an *interactive* process, children must see a *reason* to become literate. It is something they must want to work at, and the chances of that are better if they are spending time in contexts with rich, varied, and engaging literacy experiences and with adults who want to see solid progress in every child and make literacy learning fun.

During their early years, boys are more at risk for learning difficulties than girls. Soderman, Chikkara, Hsiu-Ching, and Kuo (1999) stud-

ied more than 1,000 first graders in the United States, Taiwan, and India, looking at gender differences in saccadic eye tracking of print and visual memory. They found both to be significantly related to the children's reading accuracy, and boys generally and consistently performed less well than girls. There are many other gender differences that are coming to light, according to Gurian and Stevens (2005, 48–50). We know this because, with more dopamine in their bloodstreams, boys may have a harder time sitting still in learning situations. They have an up to 25 percent smaller corpus collosum, which connects the brain hemispheres, allowing less "cross-talk" between them. In turn, there is less ability to multitask. They have weaker neural connectors in their temporal lobes, affecting sensorially detailed memory storage and listening. Thus, it is thought that boys need more sensory–tactile experience than girls for learning tasks.

In the frontal lobes, which grow more slowly in boys than girls, young males tend to be more impulsive, and in the main language centers of the brain (Broca's and Wernicke's areas in the frontal and temporal lobes), boys have later and less advanced development.

Differences in hormone levels (estrogen, oxytocin, testosterone, and vasopressin) result in a boy's lessened interest in learning through sitting and talking. There is greater aggression and competition, and boys have a greater tendency to zone out between tasks to renew, recharge, and reorient themselves.

Of course, not all gender differences result necessarily from neurobiological sources. Children's learning is also shaped by the expectations of parents and teachers and the social culture in which they grow up. Their earliest literacy experiences are influenced by what goes on at home, and there is good evidence that literacy is somewhat feminized in white, middle-class, Western homes, where boys may be taught to resist activities that might be deemed "girl appropriate." We see some of these perspectives reflected in children's early free drawing and writing, with boys more inclined to embed their narratives with cartoon figures, violent action, superheroes, and use of power and domination (Paley, 1984). Girls, conversely, are more likely to draw stylized images of children, houses, and flowers, and to develop themes around vulnerability and dependency.

What concepts should young children be developing during this earliest period in a lifetime trajectory of literacy learning? If you were to distill down the overwhelming numbers of texts, curricular and training programs, and lists of standards promoting children's emergent literacy that must come your way—and get to a bottom line about what would be reasonable for children to learn in the earliest stage of literacy—what would you say is most important? What should be included as necessary building blocks in a curriculum to ensure future literacy success or optimal development? We believe there are at least four major content areas to which we need to pay particular attention: oral language development, phonological and phonemic awareness, alphabetic principle, and **concepts of print.** You will find a number of activities to support each of these in Chapter 3.

How Does Early Literacy Emerge?

Language and literacy development are highly social in nature. Gee (2001, 31) notes that anything that has to do with oral communication involves "ways of talking, thinking, believing, knowing, acting, interacting, valuing, and feeling associated with specific socially situated identities." Similarly, behaviors involving printed words almost always involve human beings both coordinating and getting coordinated by other people. It is a "dance," it is said, with individuals playing active and passive roles, getting "in sync" with others.

From birth and prior to kindergarten, children have already begun to build their stores of information and phonological awareness that later serve as a basis for forming good, solid literacy skills. The lucky children are those who consistently see good models related to using and producing print, who are read to on a regular basis, and who have lots of opportunities to talk with people who use language effectively, correctly, and playfully. These experiences build the language strengths

that allow children to tackle the job of "symbol busting"—that is, the code-related elements of literacy: letter name knowledge, understanding the link between letters and sounds and decoding strategies, and the alphabetic principle (Barone & Morrow, 2003). Also included is recognition of punctuation, sentence grammar, and memory to organize various elements into correct sequences.

Subsequently, as they become more fluent in applying these skills and concepts, **automaticity** sets in, allowing children to recognize instantly more and more words without putting much energy into active decoding. Children can then concentrate cognitively on putting more of their energy into what the print means. At this stage, and when children have developed strong decoding skills, there is a reduction of active attention to alphabetic and phonemic aspects of print, and a greater attempt to make and receive meaning from print. Children are now equipped for rapidly expanding their vocabularies and becoming involved in more advanced reading and writing tasks.

Problems in the Pathway

There is, of course, another side to the story. Yale University researchers Sally and Bennett Shaywitz (Shaywitz, 2003) have mapped the areas of the brain involved in decoding and making sense of print—and what can go wrong when systems are not operating or developing optimally. According to Wingert and Kantrowitz (1997), children learn to read in four distinct stages (Figure 1.1). Breakdowns can occur anywhere in this process. Early warning signs during preschool and kindergarten years that a child may have a learning disability and need professional diagnosis and help include the following:

Starts talking later than other children

Has pronunciation problems

Has slow vocabulary growth

Is often unable to find the right word

Has trouble learning numbers, the alphabet, and days of the week

Has difficulty rhyming words

Is extremely restless and distractible

Has trouble interacting with peers

Displays a poor ability to follow directions or routines

Avoids puzzles, drawing, and cutting

By the end of the primary grades, girls appear to exhibit more competency in writing, write longer and more complex text, use a wider range of verbs and adjectives, and develop more descriptive and elaborate stories (Millard, 2003, 23–25). A study of first graders by Soderman and Adams (2002) indicated that six-year-old boys spent far less time involved at home in literacy activities, spent more time with their

Four Stages of Learning to Read

1. Beginning phonological awareness and an understanding that words are made up of different sounds

2. An initial knowledge of linguistics (sounds to letters) and phonics (letters to sounds), and associating those sounds with letters

3. Becoming increasingly able to match letters quickly with the appropriate sounds—that is, becoming a fast reader

4. Centering on the meaning of words

FIGURE **1.1**

Stages of Learning to Read (Wingert & Kantrowitz, 1997)

fathers in nonliteracy-related activity, and were less likely to cite literacy activities as a choice when TV or outside play was available.

All these differences have strong implications for practice in early childhood classrooms in which girls may simply be better equipped for our current heavy emphasis on literacy skill learning. It may also be true that teachers use teaching methods and activities that have more appeal to girls than to boys. These differences may also help us understand the skewed-looking percentages of males that make up those diagnosed with learning disabilities (up to 70%) and emotional impairment (up to 80%) across the United States and also in Canada, Australia, and England, where similar studies have been conducted.

The prognosis for those children who don't receive an adequate foundation in language in the preschool and kindergarten years is not good, and they are unlikely to catch up with peers in the later primary

grades. Children, and particularly boys, from low-income families are at greater risk for being ill prepared for reading instruction in the first grade and are more likely to need special education. The differences between beginning kindergarten children from lowest and highest socioeconomic status are dramatic. They are less able to recognize letters of the alphabet (85% vs. 39%), identify beginning sounds of words (51% vs. 10%), identify primary colors (90% vs. 69%), count to 20 (68% vs. 48%), or write their own name (76% vs. 54%). On average, children who come from less advantageous environments have been read to only 25 hours versus 1,000 hours for higher income children, and their accumulated experience with words is 13 million words compared with 45 million words of their peers who come from more advantaged homes (Neuman, 2006). Predictably, they constitute more of the children in our classrooms who are experiencing serious problems with reading. They will also constitute the greatest share of children who are more likely to drop out of school before graduating, develop substance abuse problems, or become juvenile offenders. Thus, we have a great deal riding on optimal literacy development in the youngest of our children.

The Whole Package: Antecedents, Transactions, and Outcomes

When we attempt to do the very best job possible in helping young children build emerging literacy skills and concepts, three major factors must be considered (Soderman et al., 2005). The first takes into consideration all the various *antecedents* children bring to the classroom, including chronological age differences, gender differences, brain organization, primary spoken language, and cultural differences.

The second factor consists of all the *transactions* related to literacy skill building that go on both inside and outside the classroom during the child's earliest years. These are influenced by how the philosophical understanding and training of their teachers and principals—their ongoing professional development and the expectations and decisions of the school district—are played out practically in the classroom day after day. Continued parental development related to literacy in both the home and school contexts is also important.

Working effectively with children in terms of literacy instruction will mean that teachers will have to work more frequently with individual children and with small groups than with the entire group. For some teachers, this will take a significant shift in practice. Opitz and Ford (2004, 394–395) indicate that one of the questions they are asked most frequently by teachers when doing staff training is what to do with the rest of the children when working with one child or a small group. Most preschool and special education teachers are expert at this and have been for a long time. They plan for well-constructed literacy-based centers that are self-sustaining, after they have demonstrated the activities in the large-group meeting just prior to the center work. After children fully understand the task, and assuming it engages their attention and can be accomplished independently or with a peer's help, interruptions for the teacher become minimal. Teachers can then draw out individual children or small groups for five- to ten-minute mini-lessons or interactions.

Second language learners face a number of unique challenges that first language children do not when beginning to read. All children who are engaged in the process of literacy code learning also require metacognitive strategies that foster **fluency** and **comprehension,** text that is matched to their reading level and interests, and extensive practice and time in reading. Second language learners automatically have a more complex job because they are likely to experience sound/symbol dissimilarity or interference, oral vocabulary constraints, limitations resulting from background knowledge, and difficulties with text structure (Lenters, 2004, 331). Given these potential snares, their teachers will want to be cautious about ever assuming that **English language learners** do not need more explicit attention to the building of vocabulary. Texts should be provided that are as close to natural speech as possible, and there should be plenty of opportunity in the classroom for oral interaction, particularly with an adult who is focused on bolstering vocabulary. Strong prereading activities, highlighted vocabulary, and repeated readings of simple, predictable texts are also helpful.

Outcomes are the third factor that must be considered. Today, given the increasing attention given to practices in early education and educational reform, these are guided by **academic standards**—in other words, what a community or school believes a child should know and do in a variety of learning domains and at particular ages. These standards have been developed by national professional organizations such as the NAEYC, the National Assessment of Educational Progress, the National Council for the Accreditation of Teachers, and the ACEI. They overlap with those developed by other organizations (e.g., the National Council of Teachers of Mathematics, the National Council of Teachers of English, and the IRA). In addition, at least 49 states have developed these standards for the elementary grades, and 30 state departments of education have developed them for children up to five years of age. All are meant to shape and improve educational quality in the implemen-

tation of a particular curriculum or program, quality of teacher preparation, and quality of the curriculum content and its assessment (Seefeldt, 2005). In other words, what teachers choose to teach, how well they teach it, the amount of time they spend on balancing directed teaching and children's practice, and how carefully they assess children's growth *do* count—and teachers are being held increasingly accountable when children fail to achieve expected outcomes. Central here is how well a child's continuous progress is monitored and shared effectively with others who can use the information to address the child's academic and developmental needs. The extent to which inputs and desired outputs are matched carefully play a critical role in each child's success (Soderman, Gregory, & McCarty, 2005).

Role of the Teacher, Administrator, and Support Staff

If you are a teacher who's been in the business for at least ten years, you will probably agree that there is more pressure on teachers today. They must be far more than content and methods specialists. The effective teacher's role includes

- Knowing child development and individual children
- Involving and collaborating with parents and families
- Planning for teaching
- Having high expectations for children
- Assessing children's learning and behavior
- Teaching for mastery
- Guiding and facilitating children's learning and behavior

In truly effective schools, however, teachers should *not* be alone in helping children learn to think more critically, to build basic skills, and to engage in socially competent behavior with others. Having knowledgeable and capable professionals on board to organize and maintain an effective learning community must be a primary consideration if we are to optimize every child's chance to become fully literate. Teachers, administrators, and support staff must exercise integrity in terms of forming connections between the academic and home settings, being good stewards of resources expended, taking responsibility for implementation of standard-based best practices on a daily basis, and continually monitoring outcomes for every child.

Sharing leadership and working together as a collegial community to keep literacy learning at the center of school activities is an approach that leads to excellent instruction and significant growth in children. This calls for commitment from every adult in the school, from the principal as instructional leader, to support staff (literacy coaches, specialists, resource teachers of bilingual or special education), to the custodian. What is shared between them in truly effective schools is a moral purpose and responsibility to create optimal learning experiences for children, with no preconceived ideas about learners on the basis of their ethnicity or socioeconomic status (Fullan, 2002).

Characteristic of this approach is that all children are expected to move ahead and experience success. Difficulties are discussed, not ignored. Informed principals are highly visible, visiting with children, teachers, and parents daily, and they walk by every classroom every day. They make short, unannounced visits to observe student learning and engagement, and then provide reflective and effective feedback to the teacher. Optimally, a risk-free environment is created in which people are working hard to do their best but may not be perfect. Student learning remains the focus, rather than "fixing" the teachers. Specialists plan and work cooperatively with classroom teachers, rather than take children "down the hall." Professionals share reading materials and other resources with one another to support good research-based instruction (Blachowicz, Obrochta, & Fogelberg, 2005; Cobb, 2005).

Lastly, the quality of children's literacy concept and skill development will rest on how well the adults in their lives exercise the following principles:

- Respect every child's ability and right to become literate.

- Design a classroom climate and learning opportunity that boosts children's motivation to learn and moves their performance in a positive direction.

- Develop learning activities that take into consideration children's cultural experience, primary spoken language, as well as cognitive, chronological, and gender differences.

- Plan activities that bring alive and advance the literacy curriculum.

- Plan literacy activities and experiences for children that are engaging, meaningful, and useful to them.

- Plan a balance of oral language, reading, and writing activities into the daily literacy block and overall schedule.

- Include time for and encourage interactions that promote collegiality and rapport, cognitive and literacy growth, and social–emotional strength.

- Provide the scaffolding support necessary to move each child ahead in skill and concept building as rigorously as possible.

- Monitor closely children's involvement in activities and understanding of the concepts to be taught.

- Implement mechanisms for getting to know children and families beyond the classroom.

- Use authentic assessment and evaluation strategies, including self-evaluation.

In this opening chapter, we provided an overview that looked at current issues in the field, some characteristics of young children in the earliest stage of emergent literacy, ways in which we believe literacy develops in the human being, potential problems that may occur in initial skill building, and the role of the teacher, administrator, and support staff in creating and providing literacy-rich learning contexts. In the chapters that follow, we look more closely at the characteristics of these contexts, activities that can be used to develop oral language and reading and writing skills, the role of parents, and strategies for effective assessment.

Chapter 2

Learning Climates and Environments That Support Best Practices in Emerging Literacy

It takes very little time when entering a school or a classroom to evaluate the learning climate and to get a "feel" for how valued children are, how much investment there is on behalf of children, and how much actual learning may be going on. In the very worst of situations, programs are rigid, relegating children to a passive role in which they are mostly learning through listening and spending time in activities that have little meaning or relevance to them. Adults are short on patience and maintain control by yelling, threatening children (counting to fives and to tens), or sending them to the principal's office. Such classrooms are frequently junk ridden or organized in a haphazard way, and ditto sheets and workbooks dominate. Children rarely make choices or function as active decision makers, and assessment of their progress is sporadic and unrelated to their classroom experiences. Parents and family members are often viewed as adversaries or as inconsequential (Kostelnik et al., 2007). These are joyless, boring places, and both children and teachers in these situations are glad when the day (and the school year) is over.

We expect that you're a teacher who thinks as much about the learning climate in your classroom as you do about academic issues. You understand that children are in process in every aspect of their development and that, as early childhood educators, we are as responsible for their abilities to function well with others in varied environments as we are responsible for teaching them to read and write well. Children's long-term literacy success depends on this. If they fail to acquire the social and self-regulatory skills they need to relate well to others in the learning environment or to become motivated to learn, we will lose them (Dickinson, McCabe, & Essex, 2006). During the early years, adults may find it more necessary to verbalize for children with limited communication skills. In the best settings, they help children develop positive social interactions, encourage them to cooperate with others, and provide a thoughtful balance between the child's need to explore independently and to learn actively from scaffolded experiences. You'll find, in such classrooms, that children with limitations are integrated into most ongoing daily activities (Harms, Clifford, & Cryer, 1998).

> *Kids can't learn much if they're not socially and emotionally comfortable in their classrooms. Although we cannot combat societal problems such as poverty, violence, and fractured families, we can, at least, do our best to make sure that when [children] are in school, they are able to experience emotional and social stability as well as academic excellence. Knowing our students well, caring about them, and valuing them [are] as important as knowing the subject matter we teach.*
>
> REGIE ROUTMAN

What Should We Expect to See?

In the best of situations, there is an immediate sense of a safe, caring, and inviting environment. Children are clearly engaged in well-constructed, collaborative activities and, for the most part, express themselves in respectful ways. There is the feeling that this classroom is definitely a good place to come to, that a sense of community and cooperation has been built, and that there is just the right balance of predictable routine and novelty (Jensen, 1998).

This is not to say that teachers in these classrooms do not encounter challenging behaviors. As in poorly run classrooms, these teachers may also deal with children who have a history of insecure attachment, a

tendency to mistrust, and a view that relationships are naturally confrontational. Poorly developed social and emotional skills are characteristic of and expected when children's earliest years have been filled with emotional distress and chaos. The difference is that the teachers who establish positive learning climates know that they often need to make an extra effort to show these children that they are valued, likable, and worth supporting—and they choose to do it through modeling, coaching, and friendly, firm guidance (Watson, 2003). They are quick to try a variety of strategies instead of relying on one "magic cure." When consequences must be applied, they are reasonable, fair, and logical, and are administered by the teacher, rather than by sending the child out of the room.

If you are interested in learning how your classroom might be viewed by an objective outsider, there are several well-designed classroom evaluation tools that we suggest:

Harms et al. (1998). *Early Childhood Environment Rating Scale—Revised Edition* (ECERS-R). This tool measures the quality of the early learning environment, including spatial, programmatic, and interpersonal features that directly affect children and adults in the setting. Seven subscales are included: space and furnishings, personal care routines, language–reasoning, activities, interaction, program structure, and parents and staff. Item scores range from 1 point (inadequate) through 7 points (excellent), and NA (not applicable). A profile can be constructed and used to compare areas of strengths and weaknesses.

Hemmeter, Maxwell, Ault, and Schuster (2001). *Assessment of Practices in Early Elementary Classrooms (APEEC).* Developed to provide a useful tool to measure K–3 general education classrooms, this tool evaluates three broad domains: physical environment, curriculum and instruction, and social context. Like the ECERS, items are formatted along a seven-point continuum with descriptors ranging from 1 to 7 points (inadequate to excellent respectively). Higher scores reflect higher quality classrooms and are correlated with positive child outcomes.

Smith and Dickenson (2002). *Early Language and Literacy Classroom Observation* (ELLCO). ELLCO examines environmental factors in prekindergarten through third grade classrooms related to early literacy and language development. It is useful for baseline assessment and subsequent progress. Of interest is whether learning environments are age appropriate, and support children's evolving interests, intentional direction of the teacher, and ability of the teacher to engage children in exploring beyond their current knowledge and skills.

Any of these instruments could be useful in evaluating how well you are creating and maintaining the learning environment in which children will spend their academic year. Rubrics are included for each of the subscales that describe inadequate to excellent learning environments for children. For example, in ECERS-R, high-quality planning for fine motor development would require rotating materials to maintain the children's interest and labeling accessible storage shelves with pictures, shapes, or colors (words for older children) to encourage self-help. Dramatic play, which greatly promotes oral language, is facilitated when themes are supported by rotated prop boxes, when props are provided that represent diversity, and when materials are provided that can continue the theme outdoors. Dramatic play is enriched when you also supply pictures and stories, and extend its content via planned field trips.

There are any number of important players or stakeholders who weave together the strands of age-appropriate, individually appropriate, and socioculturally appropriate experiences for young children in a community or school program. However, realistically, you are the most important element in determining what really happens every day. It will be your decisions that respect the unique qualities of preschool and kindergarten learners. It will be your philosophy about early education that determines how well your classroom reflects each of the ten fundamental practices considered to be essential in appropriate practice (Hart, Burts, & Charlesworth, 1997; Kostelnik et al., 2007; Miller, 2004). Rate yourself on the following:

1. *Addressing the "whole child."* How well are you meeting children's need for support in holistic development: emotional, social, cognitive, and physical?

2. *Individualizing the program to suit particular children.* Are you adapting your program planning and implementation to meet differing levels of functioning and interests of the children in your classroom?

3. *Recognizing the importance of child-initiated activity.* Do you *really* allow children in your classroom to be active decision makers in the learning process? Do you accept a wide range of constructive child responses?

4. *Recognizing the significance of play as a vehicle for learning.* Do you value play and facilitate it both indoors and outdoors?

5. *Creating flexible, stimulating classroom environments.* Are you actively promoting children's learning by using both direct and indirect instruction as appropriate?

6. *Using an integrated curriculum.* How well are you combining program and curricular areas (e.g., science, math, literacy, and social studies) in the context of daily activities?

7. *Learning by doing.* How often do you have children engaged in concrete experiences with real materials. Are the activities you plan for them useful, meaningful, and engaging?

8. *Giving children choices about what and how they learn.* Are you providing a wide range of activities and materials from which children may choose and pursue educational goals in many ways?

9. *Continually assessing individual children and the program as a whole.* There are a variety of assessment strategies, including formal and informal techniques. Are you emphasizing performance-based documentation or relying primarily on standardized instruments to learn about children's progress?

10. *Forming partnerships with family.* How well do you truly value parents and other significant family members as partners and decision makers in the education process. In what ways do you involve them?

When we make visits to preschool and kindergarten classrooms, we often are interested in documenting the types of activities that are provided for children consistently and repeatedly, understanding that the brain is a pattern-seeking organ and that children learn by practicing. We want to see certain literacy experiences for children that we *know* lead to strongly developed skills in phonological and phonemic awareness, alphabetic principle, concepts of print, and oral language. However, we are convinced that despite hours and hours of committee work to develop an appropriate literacy curriculum, the amount of training that teachers must attend, an explosion of trade books about literacy practices, and the more "rigorous" assessment practices that are now required, confusion about what should happen in good preschool and kindergarten classrooms continues. How do we get started at the beginning of the year? What is the best way to spend our minutes, hours, and days with children during the year? Of the many activities and experiences that could be used on a day-to-day basis, which ones really pay off?

Before school opens for the year, you will want to think carefully about your daily schedule, how you will introduce children to routines, the pace or speed at which the day will move, and balance that should be provided between short and long time segments, active and quiet periods, and self-directed or teacher-directed activity. Particular characteristics of the group of children you will be receiving, such as age, amount of self-control, and skill levels, should influence your planning.

The first day of school will call for leaning as much as possible on the familiar and predictable. Remember that some or many of the children may have little or no experience with routines and will not know what you expect of them. They may be frightened of being left with an unfamiliar adult in a strange setting. Having so many other children in the room at the same time may make them anxious. If possible, you may want to opt for a shortened day the first week or a slightly slower pace, shortened group time, and additional time for self-selected activity; however, you will also want to establish the general routine for what's coming in the days ahead This would be an excellent time to enlist adult volunteers who can contribute added support.

Tasks should be made as simple as possible for at least the first week of school as children become accustomed to the daily routine, each other, and you. They should be as focused as possible on the familiar and predictable, and activities should call for easy manipulation of and access to materials. Fewer activities and centers that are supplied with adequate and completely open-ended materials are preferred. For example, that a paint easel set up, rather than doing a more complicated marble painting activity. Set up a sand table and a table on which you have clay. Use crayons instead of markers, for which caps have to be replaced.

Introduce and model the proper use of materials and activities in a large group before including them in centers. Take time to *show* children how to access and return materials. Talk with them about your love of books and the way in which you take care of them. The same is true of writing and manipulative materials, use of the computer, and all other areas of the room. This will all take time at the beginning of the year, because we can't share all of this with children during the first few days. It would create cognitive overload. After you have shown children what you expect in terms of using and returning materials, reinforce appropriate behaviors and provide gentle reminders and assistance to children who lack an understanding of expected behaviors.

Structure fewer centers at the beginning of the year and gradually add more as children become increasingly adept at moving between them. Remember that too many choices may promote confusion and a lack of sustained focus in children.

As the school year progresses, make gradual changes to increase children's abilities to operate independently. Always keep your eye on children's sense of security in terms of a predictable, low-stress, and manageable environment as you do your planning.

In our work, there *are* particular activities and experiences that we see the most effective teachers using on a daily basis. They have led to the greatest skill development in young preschool and kindergarten children at the end of the year. The following checklist (Figure 2.1) is designed to have teachers rate themselves at three different periods during the school year, keeping in mind the kinds of daily activities that are proved to be best practice. These literacy activities are presented in Chapter 3; assessment activities are described in Chapter 5.

FIGURE **2.1** Teacher Self-Appraisal Checklist

Teacher Self-Appraisal: Scaffolding Emerging Literacy

Literacy Variable	Date_____	Date_____	Date_____
1. I have children sign in every day.			
2. I have children sign and date their work daily.			
3. I read aloud at least once daily, teaching several concepts of print each time.			
4. Children work in their journals daily, producing pictures and any related writing they can.			
5. I use children's printed names in some way every day.			
6. Children add a dated literacy artifact to their portfolios at least once a week.			
7. I observe one fourth to one fifth of my class each day and make anecdotal notes about their social and literacy development before leaving for the day.			
8. I have children play "literacy detective" daily with printed material.			
9. I walk the room or other contexts daily with the children, identifying letters or doing a brief sight word search.			
10. I structure at least two engaging literacy-related centers daily.			
11. I do a mini workshop on literacy skills daily for all children, teaching some aspect of the alphabetic principle, phonemic awareness, letter–sound association, letter–grapheme association, and concept of print.			

(continues)

FIGURE **2.1** *(Continued)*

Literacy Variable	Date_____	Date_____	Date_____
12. I sing familiar songs or recite familiar nursery rhymes, poems, or finger plays with children daily.			
13. I have at least a brief conversation with each child each day to develop a rapport and extend their oral language skills.			
14. Children in my room have plenty of opportunities to talk with one another daily.			
15. I teach children one new vocabulary word each day and post it on the word wall or a concept chart.			
16. I help children focus on a listening or viewing skill each day.			
17. Daily, I model and encourage good communication skills, such as complete sentences, good eye contact, clear speech, and correct grammar.			
18. Daily, I model an aspect of writing skill to children, using such activities as morning message, sharing the pen, predictable charts, attribute naming, and so forth.			
19. Daily, I include a phonemic awareness activity (e.g., syllabification, onset and rime) in my instruction.			
20. My classroom is clean and well organized, print rich, and structured so that children can easily and independently access and return materials.			

Managing Children Effectively: Creating an Atmosphere of Trust and Support

By the end of the preschool years, most children have become somewhat capable of managing their everyday emotional experiences. In addition to the basic emotions, they now are aware of feeling pride, shame, guilt, and embarrassment. They can anticipate others' emotions enough to adjust their own behavior, and they've even begun to hide their own emotions from others (Shonkoff & Phillips, 2000).

The young child's basic needs are not any different from the basic needs we all have: belonging, power, freedom, and fun. According to William Glasser (1998), the most important of these is the need for identity or sense of belonging. Good teachers provide this by quickly learning and using children's names, greeting them individually at the beginning of the day, and having additional conversations with them during the day. These teachers provide personal space for each child, make connections to the children's real world, and let children know they've been missed when they're absent. These teachers enhance children's sense of power by giving them learning choices, involving them in decision making (such as helping to construct the classroom rules), letting them know when changes are coming up, assigning genuine responsibility for maintaining the classroom, and recognizing their achievements. Children in such classrooms have the freedom to make mistakes as long as they are trying their best. They have the freedom to go to the bathroom when they want and are allowed time within the day to make self-selected learning choices as long as they are acting responsibly. Teachers like these talk about how everyone is good at something; highlight successes for every child; take delight in being in the moment with the children; are occasionally silly; use kind, gentle humor to diffuse tension; and teach children to give encouragement and compliments to one another. There is no room in these classrooms for bullying, sarcasm, or disrespect—on the part of adults or children.

A positive verbal environment is purposefully planned and maintained at all times, ensuring that children experience socially rewarding interactions with the adults in the setting. In classrooms like these, it's easy to see that fundamental attitudes of affection, interest, and involvement with children predominate on the part of every adult. Children appear at ease and secure in these settings, and observers are apt to see adults adhering to the following ten principles:

1. Actively engaging with the children, saving social interactions with other adults for when children are not present

2. Using language to demonstrate their interest in children by reflecting on what the children are doing, noticing children's accomplishments, laughing along with the children, answering their questions, and acknowledging their comments

3. Actively listening to children, replying thoughtfully to their ideas, accepting their ideas, remembering to follow up later on, and inviting children to elaborate on their ideas

4. Speaking courteously to children, allowing them to complete their thoughts without interrupting them, demonstrating patience, using an accepting tone of voice, and modeling social amenities such as please, thank you, and excuse me

5. *Discussing children* professionally by avoiding the labeling of children or their families and discussing issues in private only with appropriate parties

6. Communicating informally with children throughout the day, focusing on individual children and their current needs and interests

7. Using children's ideas and interests to guide the conversation, following up on children's leads in conversations, bringing up subjects they know will be interesting to individual children, using **open-ended questions** (Why do you think . . . ?) and thought-provoking questions

8. Using children's names in positive circumstances (never in place of negative commands)

9. Using words to guide children's behavior—to encourage, to assist with stress management, to help children change their behavior without damaging their self-esteem

10. Using praise sincerely and constructively; delivering individual, sincere compliments that describe the child's accomplishment; focusing on positive behavior and never putting others down. (Kostelnik, Whiren, Soderman, & Gregory, 2006, 106–107)

In all these ways, effective teachers quickly develop a rapport with each child so that the child feels valued in the classroom setting and, in turn, begins to value the teacher's opinion. Following these guidelines consistently will increase your ability to help misbehaving children become more cooperative and productive, because your disapproval will actually mean something to the child. It is something the child comes to avoid because it is not as enjoyable as your approval and positive acknowledgment that is earned through better behavioral choices.

When a child steps outside of acceptable behavior, it should not be ignored. The child's point of view should be acknowledged; however, make it very clear to the child the behavior that is problematic and why it is a problem. Involve the child in opting for a better choice and let the child know the consequences of choosing not to behave appropriately. No excuses are accepted for the child not following through, and consequences are applied swiftly without subsequent warning, counting, nagging, or preaching if the child does not comply. When this kind of climate is established, even troubled children have a better chance of regulating their own behavior and emotions in a more positive direction.

We often sing with young children the song, "If you're happy and you know it clap your hands. If you're happy and you know it clap your hands. If you're happy and you know it, and you really want to show it, if you're happy and you know it clap your hands." When children come into classrooms where teachers mirror and model joy, delight, excitement, enthusiasm, and other positive emotions without being falsely cheerful, children learn they can do that as well. They also know that when they need to express their sadness, fear, anger, worry, and loneliness, there will be someone who can be relied on who is genuinely helpful and interested, someone who infuses the classroom with the "social strength necessary to accommodate the expression of negative as well as positive affects" (Koplow, 1996, 24–25). We're hoping all children can have teachers like this because they need them to grow up to be strong, caring adults.

Embracing Classroom Diversity and Providing Support for English Language Learners

Each of us, through our language, our thinking, and our approach to children and families from diverse backgrounds, needs to reflect how we want the future to be—like a vivid, rich and colorful display of autumn foliage. The community of early childhood professionals is gifted with a unique opportunity.

We are in a position to have a lasting influence on young children's attitudes toward linguistic and cultural diversity. Unlike the children we care for and educate, we are change agents.

JOSUE CRUZ, JR., PRESIDENT OF NAEYC

In our early childhood laboratories at Michigan State University, we serve a highly diverse population of families and children who speak a number of languages. These include Spanish, Korean, Chinese (Cantonese and Mandarin), Japanese, Arabic, African, Polish, and Russian. Within these languages, several dialects may be spoken. Many of the children and families do not speak English on entry into the program, and the faculty and students in the laboratories are committed to promoting as positive an outcome for these children as they do for others who enter school with English as their primary language. In doing so, and to the extent possible, we observe the following performance standards now being required of all Head Start programs in broadly supporting English language learners and families (David, 2005, 40):

- Provide an environment of acceptance that supports and respects gender, culture, age, language, ethnicity, and family composition

- Serve foods that reflect cultural and ethnic preferences

- Communicate with families in their preferred or primary language, or through an interpreter, to the extent feasible

- Hire staff, whenever possible, who speak the home languages of the enrolled children and, when a majority of children speak the same language, hire at least one classroom staff member or home visitor who speaks their language

■ Promote family participation in literacy-related activities in both English and the home language

Because we operate within the context of a university, we have available to us resources such as the Michigan State University Speech and Language Clinic, as well as students and faculty from other countries who speak both fluent English and other languages. Student teachers in the program who speak the language of one or more of the English language learners in the program have translated familiar songs such as the birthday song. They have then taught these songs to all children in the laboratories so that they can help children who are learning English celebrate on special days. However, we rely just as much on relationships we have built in communities surrounding the greater Lansing area to provide support for English language learning aspects of our program. Many adults coming from non-English-speaking populations have created support groups and identified bilingual persons within the group who are willing to serve as volunteers and translators of language and cultural norms for childcare centers, school systems, and other community organizations. Teachers within Lansing public schools rely on these liaisons as much as we do.

Realistically, because there are as many as 140 or more different languages now spoken in the United States, communities and school systems may not be able to have available someone who speaks the child's or family's primary language. This may be a greater challenge in rural communities than in urban centers. However, there are a number of strategies that can be used to make sure that children are as comfortable as possible and that they move along as well as possible in terms of their overall development.

A primary task, if you have children in your classroom who speak little English, if at all, is to build a rudimentary English vocabulary as quickly as possible. This is best accomplished in active classrooms where English language learners hear plenty of conversation between adults and children, and among their peers. Targeted vocabulary expansion efforts are often done by

repeatedly naming people, common objects, and frequently seen actions in the classroom. Scaffolding experiences are purposefully structured, taking children from where they are functioning independently to new levels of understanding and skill development. Reflection is a natural part of the way adults interact with children to help all children build language and articulation skills. In one instance, a student teacher who was watching a child put together a puzzle stopped to say, "Assefa, you like doing puzzles! You've chosen your favorite one about transportation. I see [pointing to each one] an airplane, a fire engine, a spaceship, and a boat in the puzzle. We saw a fire engine last week when we went to the firehouse. Show me the fire engine!" The child then pointed to the fire engine, looked up shyly, grinned, and said, "Fire engine!"

It wasn't surprising to see Assefa later drawing the fire engine, which the teacher helped him label. Still later in the morning, as Assefa found his name tag at the snack table, the teacher had each child at the table point to his or her name tag, say his or her name, and then had the rest of the children at the table repeat that name and chant the letters in the child's name. As children chanted the letters in Assefa's name, everyone saw his familiar grin again. This is an activity in which children can fully participate and enjoy, because children's names are used often in the classroom for varied literacy experiences. With lots of experiences like this every day, young children learn English amazingly quickly.

Graves and Fitzgerald (2003) note that scaffolding was originally used to characterize mothers' verbal interaction when reading to their young children. They write:

> For example, in sharing a picture book with a child and attempting to assist the child in reading the words that identify the pictures, a mother might at first simply page through the book, familiarizing the child with the pictures and general content of the book. Then she might focus on a single picture and ask the child what it is. After this, she might point to the word below the picture, tell the child that the word names the picture, ask the child what the word is, and provide him or her with feedback on the correctness of the answer. The important point is that the mother has neither simply told the child the word nor simply asked him or her to say it. Instead, she has built an instructional structure, a scaffold, that assists the student in learning. (97)

It is helpful to have available in the classroom one of the many picture dictionaries of common English words. These can be paged through for a few minutes each day with a child, centering especially on more common objects in the classroom. You might simply page slowly through the book, allowing the child to spot objects he or she knows and can name. This can also help enormously when a child is confused about something that a simple picture might clarify.

Other strategies that we've provided in another of our texts (Soderman et al., 2005, 7) include learning as much as possible about the child's linguistic, cultural, and educational backgrounds. What is the child's full name and how is it written in his or her home language? What name does the child prefer for classroom use? Who are the persons who live with the child at home, and what are their names? Which language is preferred for oral communication at home? In what language are there written materials in the house? Are there any special dietary, clothing, or religious requirements that must be observed?

Use the child's native language if at all possible for clarification of vocabulary, directions, or key concepts. Provide think-alouds and modeling when explaining an upcoming activity. Also, provide learning strategies, such as tapping the child's prior knowledge, using visuals and manipulatives, and teaching key vocabulary. Adjust your speech, face the child when speaking, pause more frequently, paraphrase, use shorter sentences, increase waiting time for children to answer, and always focus on the child's meaning, rather than on grammar (Laturnau, 2003).

With the help of the child's parents or an interpreter, make an effort to learn at least a few words in the child's language, such as "Good morning," "Show me," "Good job," and "See you tomorrow." You may want to label areas of the classroom in the child's language or incorporate names of the child's family members into the stories you tell (Smyth, 2003).

We believe that art, music, and choral reading are tremendously helpful in supporting ways for English language learners to express their ideas and build English skills. Their artwork, what they choose to draw freely or construct with clay and other materials, becomes a window into what is important to them and what they are thinking. Art is a linking language between the English they are learning to understand and their primary language, which has suddenly become less useful to them in their new context. Music offers relief, particularly when they

can sing or chant along with other children. There's enough noise that
if they make a mistake or don't know the words, no one notices.
Children can participate by humming and then throwing in the occa-
sional known word until familiarity and skill take over. The same thing
is true in **choral or echo reading,** during which the teacher reads a line
and children repeat it. All these activities provide fun and relief from
the stress that an English learner must constantly feel in a setting in
which almost everyone else has the necessary skills to communicate,
skills that are only in process for them.

Children who are English-language learners can easily get lost in
the busy life of an early childhood classroom, making regular, appropriate assessment a critical factor. We need to make sure they are growing in their literacy abilities and acculturation in our classrooms. Ideas
about how to assess the English language learners' progress are also
found in Chapter 5.

Facilitating Learning: Organizing Space, Materials, Time, and Routines

The physical attractiveness of an early childhood classroom, the way
the teacher and children care for materials and equipment, and how
time and routines are structured all have a positive or negative effect
on the quality of the instructional program and overall learning climate. Classrooms should be arranged to facilitate quiet and efficient
movement, and to help children access and return materials easily and
independently. A room that is organized, not crowded, and free from
piles of junk or infrequently used equipment allows children to focus
on their work. There should never be materials present that children
are not allowed to touch. Good storage, color-coded and labeled materials on open shelves, child-size tables and chairs, clean furnishings,
and equipment that is in good repair are all compatible with good
learning opportunities.

When considering the kinds of materials and equipment that are
needed to operate the classroom in a comfortable way (Figure 2.2),
teachers often have to find ways to supplement those provided by the
school—and they do! For example, Gilberto Sanchez asked parents of

Color-coded and labeled materials

Child-size tables and chairs

Storage near well-constructed literacy interest centers

A minimum of commercially produced print

Plenty of children's work on display at their eye level

A posted schedule

Large and small whiteboards and dry-erase markers

Pocket charts so that children can match print

Inviting literacy materials and equipment in all centers, as well as outdoors

Eye-level word wall

Ten to twelve sets of movable letters

One hundred or more narrative and expository picture books of different genres (4 to 20 books per child) and other printed materials such as comic books, class-made books, big books, magazines, catalogs, menus, wordless picture books, job charts, and books in the other languages represented in the classroom

Computers and well-chosen software

Audio- and videotapes, tape recorder, and headphones

Lots of varied writing tools and materials

A laminator

Dramatic play and storytelling props

Puppets

Flannel board and flannel board stories

Musical instruments, songbooks and charts, CDs, and tapes

Clipboards

Picture, letter, and word matching games

Puzzles and manipulatives

Science materials (magnifying glasses, magnets, scales, measuring tools)

Easels and newsprint

Blocks and supporting materials

Telephones and telephone books

Polaroid and digital cameras

Sign-in and sign-up sheets

Large-print dictionaries, globe, encyclopedia, and atlas

Alphabet strips, alphabet cards, and word cards

Signs, lists, concept charts, interactive charts, and labels

Letter boxes containing letter-connected objects

Art materials

the Hispanic children in his classroom if they would help him gather some engaging picture books written in Spanish. They came through! Glenna DeFord works regularly with the children's librarian in her town to check out an armload of relevant books monthly that have to do with ongoing projects and children's interests. Friends of the library pay attention to and support Glenna's needs in the purchases they make yearly. Glenna also finds small grants to purchase needed equipment.

In our best early childhood classrooms, there are well-constructed interest centers, including a quiet area. There is a minimum of commercially produced print, and plenty of children's work is displayed at their eye level. Attention is given to location and proximity of related interest areas. For example, the writing center is located in front of the word wall, next to the storage of books and a quiet area for reading.

We recently visited Lynne Munson's classroom in Kalamazoo, Michigan. She is a preschool teacher in Kalamazoo's excellent Early Reading First program. She works with 18 children in a well-paced day, filled with engaging activities to promote children's **phonological awareness,** alphabetic awareness, oral language, and concepts of print. The room is large, clean, and well organized. Time is provided for lap reading with the children, singing familiar songs, and creative use of nursery rhymes. Print and print opportunities are found in every area of the room, but it doesn't just exist: It's easy to see that Lynne has staged the environment so that children are caught by the print in very special ways. When she is working with the children in large or small groups, she helps them develop positive listening and attending behaviors by using signals such as, "Look over here," "I'm going to look carefully right here," and "Be thinking about what comes next, but don't let it come out of your mouths yet," and "Now, let me think [she pauses]. How does the story begin?" The children

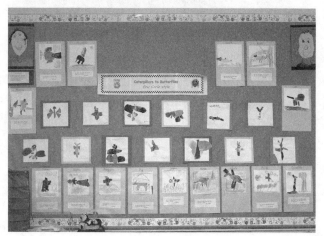

respond well, "playing the game" that she suggests. Her voice is soft and natural, sending a signal to the children that she does not need or intend to talk over them, and she expects them to listen when others are talking. When they don't, she warmly reminds them not to interrupt, but comes back to a child who had something to add. She knows how important it is for children to express themselves, and she allows plenty of opportunities for them to share communication time and space in the classroom. In dismissing them from a large group so that they can work independently, she uses their names to promote a literacy concept. Adding to this, she asks them to tell the group (not just her) where they are going that morning in a whole sentence. "Tell me the whole thing," she says with a smile, and children proudly do so: "I am going to work in the housekeeping area." Each child carries a "ticket" with a loop on it that they hang on one of the hooks Lynne has at each of the centers, controlling the number of children using the centers at any one time. As children work in the well-structured centers, Lynne is up and about the room, stopping briefly to facilitate new understandings, helping children problem solve in positive ways, and reinforcing particular concepts: "Oh, Stephen, I see you are making a shape person and you've already written your name on your paper. Good that you remembered that." Even when stopping to interact briefly with an individual child or small group of children, she maintains a global view of the classroom. She carries with her a clipboard on which she has a grid with each child's name, and she often takes time to make a notation about an observation she has made. She uses these notes later to document the kinds of skills she wants to see as outcomes for these children who will spend the school year with her.

A daily schedule is posted and adhered to, but small adaptations are made in relation to children's interests and abilities to engage in structured activities. Small-group and individualized work by children is predominant in Lynne's classroom, rather than whole-group instruction. Blocks of time allow for uninterrupted focus on particular curricular areas. The pace of the morning allows children to complete expected work without undue stress or boredom, and it's obvious that there is recognition in planning for variations and differences in children's abilities, attention spans, and learning styles. A balanced schedule allows for short and long time segments, active and quiet periods, and self-directed and teacher-directed activity. More often than not, Lynne has organized children into heterogeneous groups in terms of ability, cultural differences, gender, and race. This allows for greater cross-fertilization of learning and sharing of ideas, abilities, and talents.

Sound perfect or impossible? It's not. Lynne is very real, and there is evidence of many such smoothly run and productive classrooms like hers. At the end of the session or day in these classrooms, it's always obvious that good work has been accomplished in promoting children's literacy and social competence. Children walk out richer in some way than when they entered, and Lynne knows it. That makes the extra effort that she puts into preparation and ongoing care of the classroom and children well worth it. The purpose of thinking so carefully about the overall learning climate and environment is to set the stage for growth-producing interaction among the players in the classroom space—the children and teacher who will work together for an entire year to master certain learning goals. With teachers like Lynne, there's almost always satisfaction at the end of the day (or the year) that things went pretty well, that her work is important in terms of the children's futures, and that she is putting into practice the best teaching and learning strategies we know in early childhood education.

Structuring Effective Literacy Learning Centers

Providing genuine choices for children means providing effective learning centers each day in which they can work for at least an hour a day. Opitz and Ford (2004) suggest the following resources for teachers who want to become more effective in structuring their teaching this way:

Diller, D. (2003). *Literacy work stations: Making centers work.* Portland, ME: Stenhouse.

Finney, S. (2003). *Independent activities that keep kids learning . . . while you teach small groups.* New York: Scholastic.

Nations, S., & Alonso, M. (2001). *Primary literacy centers: Making reading and writing STICK!* Gainesville, FL: Maupin House.

In preschools and kindergartens, it would be inappropriate not to include such centers as a place to convene the total group, conduct dramatic play; provide blocks, sand, and water; and incorporate mathematics and science, art, and language arts (listening, writing, reading, viewing). Each should attract and sustain children's interest, and there should be continuous oversight by the teacher about which centers are chosen by children and which are ignored or avoided.

The purpose of a center can be posted at the site, so that parents and other visitors can become more aware of its usefulness. For example, one teacher who felt that she had to defend the inclusion of her "Pretend Center" hung the following near the center: *This Pretend Center offers children opportunities to act out real-life experiences, expand their perspectives of what others think and roles they play, practice their social skills, and expand their vocabularies. What other skill do you see developing?* She left a number of lines for responses from classroom visitors, and a couple of them had actually penned in these ideas:

> The children are developing their leadership and following skills. _____
>
> They're practicing what it will be like to be a grown-up. _____
>
> Two children are trying to spell words for a grocery list. _____

What we saw when we observed were five children who were taking advantage of this time to suspend reality. A "husband and wife" were on the two telephones in the area, talking about the fact that the "baby was sick." We noticed a telephone book, paper and pencils that had been supplied for note making and taking, a copy of yesterday's newspaper, and two magazines the teacher had placed on the table. The children had on costumes they had devised from the assorted scarves, pieces of lace curtain, jackets, hats, and jewelry provided, and from the look on their faces, they were all "very concerned" about the situation. Another child was playing the part of the doctor and was writing a "subscription" for the baby. No one wanted to play the baby, which was represented by a doll wrapped in a towel. The classroom aide, hearing about the "subscription," stopped by to deliver a new pad of yellow sticky notes to the doctor for the "prescriptions" he was writing. "Did you need this *prescription* pad for the *prescriptions* you're writing?" she asked. Two other children were simply making and serving food, unaware or unconcerned that they were operating their restaurant in the same space that was also a home and a doctor's office.

Although there are a lot of obvious social connections that are being made in this particular center, and language ones as well, other skills and concepts that will be useful to these children later on in their literacy ventures may not be as obvious. We believe these include more sophisticated imagination and abstract thinking abilities, better ability to see themes in what they will later read, and better recognition of the elements in stories and plays (story line, characters, events, problems, solutions, settings, plots, beginning and endings, the shaping of dialog). We see these early experiences as instrumental in children being able to

do oral presentations with confidence, **reader's theater** and other creative dramatics, as well as **story retelling.**

We hope we're not stretching this too far, but we believe that in our current push toward formal reading and writing for young children, we may have forgotten some of the prerequisites in early childhood that need to be practiced to set the stage. Like the disappearance of nursery rhymes in lots of homes today in favor of the ever-present videos and cartoons, "playing house" (school, store, and so on) may not be as opportune for children as in the past. We recognize what is lost in terms of phonological awareness when nursery rhymes are not experienced, and so we try to make up for it by focusing heavily on them in early childhood education settings. We may also want to take a step back to consider what very young children may lose when time is no longer allocated to a "nonacademic" curriculum or is shortened in lieu of other "more important" priorities on adult agendas.

The quality of the language center itself is crucial in terms of children choosing to participate on a voluntary basis. Studies have indicated that placing an adult volunteer in this center automatically results in children spending more sustained time in the center, choosing to have the adult read a book, and choosing to look at books themselves for a longer period of time than when a volunteer is not stationed in the center. Comfortable places to sit, besides the floor, make the center more attractive to children. Displaying the covers of books rather than just a spine, or placing them in a basket also draws children. This is a place where you will logically want to combine reading and writing. It should be large enough to contain one or two computers so that children begin to connect the power of computers to writing and reading and not just playing games. It should also contain a place where tapes of familiar books can be stored by the books, with more than one set of headphones for children who want to listen to the story. Rather than purchasing these tapes, you can make them yourself, because children will love listening to your familiar voice reading the story "just to them." A bell or chime can be inserted into the taped story so that children are alerted to turn the page. A flannel board can be placed on the floor, with a basket of manila envelopes filled with familiar flannel board story pieces and the book itself. Similarly, there can be a table on which a basket has been placed, filled with manila envelopes containing five to seven pictures of events in a familiar story that can be sequenced by the children on the tabletop. The book should also be included in the envelope so that children can check their sequence or use it to replicate the sequence.

At the writing center, include lots of writing materials and also "interesting" equipment, such as an old typewriter, a stapler, stamps and stamp pads, stickers, tracing materials, envelopes, a class-made dictionary, a large-print picture dictionary, copies of the children's names and often-used words on the word wall, an unfettered alphabet in upper- and lower-case, and concept charts with a web of words related to anything being studied by the children. Class-made books will be a favorite here, and the daily morning message or predictable chart should be standing nearby on an easel so that children can read it with a peer. Pat Schulze, head teacher in Michigan State University's Child Development Laboratory, keeps a list of classmate's names at the writing center for the children's easy reference.

There is not enough space here to describe completely what should go into a language arts center; besides, our ideas might not be as rich or as applicable as those you might come up with. The bottom line is that for preschool and kindergarten children who are discovering the wonders of print, you must strive to make the language arts center wonderful. It should be a cornerstone of activity in the early childhood classroom.

Selecting Books for Your Literacy-Rich Classroom

Today, there are any number of organizations and publishers who have done the job of sequencing books from easiest, predictable, and repetitive text to more challenging selections. These books can be color coded and placed in baskets or on accompanying color-coded shelves for children's independent use. Should we be doing this with preschool and kindergarten children? We think it would be unnecessary and even inappropriate at this stage of emerging literacy. There are some guidelines, however, for choosing the kinds of books to offer for independent use by the children and also for reading to children. Four guidelines offered by Bennett–Armistead, Duke, and Moses (2005, 131) are to evaluate quality and appropriateness by the number of words (few on the page for very young children and more for older), artwork and language (select books with rich illustrations and excellent photos so that children can discuss and draw meaning from them, particularly when "reading" independently), topic (familiarity and interest are important here), and physical format (durability, nontoxic). Probably a good rule of thumb is to select books that have one line of print on each page per age of the child. For those of you who are teaching older preschoolers and kindergarten children, you will want to choose books with great illustrations and three to six lines of print per page.

Some packaged curricula come with highly predictable and repetitive books for use with beginning readers. They are purposefully limited in vocabulary, and although we are not opposed to their use along with good literature, we would strongly recommend that they not be the only books that are read or offered to children. One of the very good reasons for reading to children is that it broadens their vocabulary and development of concepts about people and the world considerably. Well-written children's books contain vocabulary that we rarely hear in everyday conversation between people—words like *menagerie, cautionary, prancing,* and *proclamation.* They take children on imagination journeys that require more sophisticated language and build their abilities to later decode words they will meet in the texts they read.

We would urge you to be highly selective about the literature you choose to read and make available to children. This could vary from year to year, depending on the particular interests of the children.

Do they love it when you read to them the delightful poems of Jack Prelutsky, such as *Awful Ogre's Awful Day?* If so, they may also enjoy Prelutsky's *The Frogs Wore Red Suspenders* and *The Dragons Are Singing.* Crystal Bowman's *If Peas Could Taste Like Candy,* Alan Katz's *Take Me out of the Bathtub,* and Douglas Florian's *Insectlopoedia* are also wonderful. When you display information books on transportation and construction in the block center, including classics such as Virginia Burton's *Mike Mulligan and His Steam Shovel* and Paul Strickland's *Big Dig,* does the play of the children become more involved and exciting? Does this year's class really like taking part in interactive reading with you and then copy that with each other, using such predictable books such as *Brown Bear, Brown Bear, What Do You See?* If so, you want to have several of them available in the book corner in addition to using them in large and small groups.

Include **wordless books,** such as Alexandra Day's *Good Dog Carl* and *Carl's Birthday.* After paging silently through the book, go back and have children create and verbalize scripts that tell what Carl is doing. Use ABC and concept books for lap reading, such as *Museum ABC* from New York's Metropolitan Museum of Art, Sleeping Bear Press' *W is for Wind: A Weather Alphabet* by P. Michaels, and the many wonderful Gale Gibbons's books, *Polar Bears, Penguins, Sharks,* and *The Pumpkin Book,* so that you can test the child's knowledge informally while enjoying a read-aloud together. Stock different versions of *Three Pigs* and *Three Bears* books so that children can compare illustrators and versions of the story.

When making your choices about which books to include in your classroom, remember children who have special needs and those who are English language learners. Marcus Pfister's *The Rainbow Fish* is now published in a number of different languages, thrilling children from other countries when they find it on the table along with the English version. In response to the number of English language learners currently populating our schools, bookstores are now carrying lovely new books such as *My Name Is Yoon* by Helen Recorvits, the story of a child from Korea who finds herself as an English language learner in a new school.

Children in early childhood classrooms clearly enjoy long-time favorites, especially some that are read to them at home or those that come in big-book format. Moore and Lyon (2005) have listed a number of these, and some from their list that we especially enjoy are:

Mrs. Wishy-Washy (J. Cowley)

A Pocket for Corduroy (D. Freeman)

Rosie's Walk (P. Hutchins)

Brown Bear, Brown Bear, What Do You See? (B. Martin)

Wheels on the Bus and Baby Beluga (Raffi)

Curious George Goes to the Hospital (Rey & Rey)

We're Going on a Bear Hunt (M. Rosen)

The True Story of the 3 Little Pigs (J. Scieszka)

I Know an Old Lady Who Swallowed a Fly (S. Taback)

The Bear Went over the Mountain (R. L. Williams)

At Michigan State, in our preservice teacher training curriculum class, we have students select a children's picture book and then develop spin-off activities in every domain (science, math, social, emotional, physical, language) that relate to the book. These can then be implemented in the early childhood classroom so that children begin to see relationships in what they are learning. Books they especially like for this purpose are:

Gingerbread Baby (J. Brett)

Strega Nona (T. de Paola)

Make Way for Ducklings (R. McClosky)

The Snowy Day (E. Keats)

One Fine Day (N. Hogrogian)

Where the Wild Things Are (M. Sendak)

The Little House (V. Burton)

The Napping House (A. Wood)

Rumplestiltskin (P. Zelinsky)

Stone Soup (M. Brown)

For the past 13 years, the IRA and the Children's Book Council have published an annual list of choices made by 10,000 schoolchildren from different regions of the United States. The selections come from books published the prior year and the entries are then reviewed by teams of literature specialists, classroom teachers, school librarians, and children. An annotated list may be found in the October, 2005, *Reading Teacher*. Categorical levels include beginning readers, young readers, and advanced readers. The IRA also publishes a list of ideas for making the most of the books, *Celebrating Children's Choices: 25 Years of Children's Favorite Books* (2000, ISBN 0-87207-276-2), which is a collection of classroom applications. You can share this list with parents who are wondering what books to buy as a gift for the classroom or for their own children, community organizations that might like to purchase new books for the school, or school committees that have some funding to supply new books. This year's selections included the beginning reader choices shown in Figure 2.3.

FIGURE **2.3** Children's favorite New Books for Beginning Readers, 2005

Title	Author	Illustrator	ISBN
Actual Size	S. Jenkins	Author	0-618-37594-5
All Year Long	K. W. Deady	L. Bronson	1-57505-537-6
And Here's To You!	D. Elliott	R. Cecil	0-7636-1427-0
Baby Brains: The Smartest Baby in the Whole World	S. James	Author	0-7636-2507-8
Beach Day!	P. Lakin	S. Nash	0-8037-2894-8
Beatrice Doesn't Want To	L. Numeroff	L. Munsinger	0-7636-1160-3
The Beetle Alphabet Book	J. Pallotta	D. Biedrzycki	1-57091-551-2
The Best Cat in the World	L. Newman	R. Himler	0-8028-5252-1
Big Week for Little Mouse	E. Fernandes	K. Fernandes	1-555337-665-X
Billy Tibbles Moves Out!	J. Fearnley	Author	0-06-054560-6
Boom Chicka Rock	J. Archambault	S. Chitwood	0-399-3-23587-6
The Cat Who Walked Across France	K. Banks	G. Hallensleben	0-374-39968-9
Clatter Bash! A Day of the Dead Celebration	R. Keep	Author	1-56145-304-8
Cock-a-Doodle Moooo! A Mixed-up Menagerie	K. DuQuette	Author	0-399-23889-1
The Copy Crocs	D. Bedford	E. Bolam	1-56145-304-8
The Daddy Mountain	J. Feiffer	Author	0-7868-0912-4
Daffodil	E. Jenkins	T. Bogacki	0-374-31676-7
Dear Tooth Fairy	A. Durant	V. Cabban	0-7636-2175-7
Don't Forget to Come Back!	R. Harris	H. Bliss	0-7636-1782-2
Drumheller Dinosaur Dance	R. Heidbreder	B. Slavin and E. Melo	1-55337-393-6
Enrico Starts School	C. Middleton	Author	0-8037-3017-9

FIGURE **2.3** *(Continued)*

Title	Author	Illustrator	ISBN
Fairytale News	C. and J. Hawkins	Authors	0-7636-2166-8
Four Boys Named Jordan	J. Harper	T. C. King	0-399-23711-9
The Friend	S. Stewart	D. Small	0-374-32463-8
Gator Gumbo: A Spicy-Hot Tale	C. Fleming	S. A. Lambert	0-374-38050-3
Goldilocks and the Three Martians	S. Smith	M. Garland	0525-46972-9
Here They Come!	D. Costello	Author	0-374-33051-4
Hot Hot Hot	N. Layton	Author	0-37636-2148-X
How to Catch a Star	O. Jeffers	Author	0-399-24286-4
I Am TOO Absolutely Small for School	L. Child	Author	0-7636-2403-9
It's Bedtime, Wibbly Pig	M. Inkpen	Author	0-670-05880-7
Knuffle Bunny: A Cautionary Tale	M. Willems	Author	0-7868-1870-0
Larabee	K. Luthardt	Author	1-56145-300-5
Mister Seahorse	E. Carle	Author	00-399-24269-a4
Most Loved Monster	L. Downey	J. E. Davis	0-8037-2728-3
No Laughing, No Smiling, No Giggling	J. Stevenson	Author	0-374-31829-8
Our Principal Promised to Kiss a Pig	K. Dakos and A. DesMarteau	C. DiRocco	0-807a5-6629-2
Over the Hills & Far Away	C. Conover	Author	0-374-38043-0
The Pig Who Went Home on Sunday: An Appalachian Folktale	D. Davis	J. Mazzucco	0-87483-571-2
Prancing, Dancing Lily	M. D. Arnold	J. Manders	0-8037-2660-0
Rooster Can't Cock-a-Doodle-Doo	K. Rostoker–Gruber	P. R. deTagyos	0-8037-2877-8

(continues)

FIGURE **2.3** *(Continued)*

Title	Author	Illustrator	ISBN
Show Dog	M. McCarthy	Author	0-670-03688-9
Smudge Bunny	B. Siegel	L. J. Bryant	1-932073-03-5
Someone Bigger	J. Emmett	A. Reynolds	0-618-44397-5
Stinky Smelly Feet: A Love Story	M. Palatini	E. Long	0-525-47201-0
Super Sam!	L. Ries	S. Rama	1-58089-041-5
Ten Redneck Babies: A Southern Counting Book	D. Davis	S. M. Ward	1-58980-232-2
That Dancin' Dolly	J. Merz	Author	0-525-47214-2
This Is the Teacher	R. G. Green	M. Lester	0-525-47125-1
Tigress	N. Dowson	J. Chapman	0-7636-2325-3
Truck Duck	M. Rex	Author	0-399-24009-8
Walter the Farting Dog: Trouble at the Yard Sale	W. Katzwinkel and G. Murray	A. Colman	0-525-47217-7
What's That Awful Smell?	H. Tekavec	M. Spengler	0-8037-2660-0
Who Will Tuck Me in Tonight?	C. Roth	V. Gorbachev	0-7358-1773-1
Widget and the Puppy	L. Rossiter McFarland	J. McFarland	0-374-38429-0
Worm Gets a Job	K. Caple	Author	0-7636-1694-X

Role of the Community in Creating Literacy-Rich Contexts for Young Children

Excellent preschools and kindergartens can be found in almost any European country today, and in countries in many other parts of the world. Even those with few resources are recognizing the importance of providing high-quality early childhood education and funneling scarce resources in that direction.

There has been a long-held perspective in the United States that local educational autonomy should be maintained. If this is to remain true, but also remain in the best long-range interests of children, local school systems and communities will have to take more responsibility for making sure that even the youngest have available what they need at the start.

In our communities, adults must come together to evaluate comprehensive educational opportunities for children. They must consider fairly whether early childhood educators are deemed as important as others in the grand scheme of an excellent education, whether they are paid as well as others to avoid turnover, whether they have planning time built into their schedules, whether buildings and classrooms provided for young children are in good repair and attractive, and whether teachers have enough materials to teach well without having to spend large amounts of their own salary to do so. School systems must consider whether preschool staff are part of "the regular faculty" or just an appendage. Genuine, useful, and respectful linkages must be developed in which early education curriculum and assessment are included in the scope and sequence presented by the schools. Knowledgeable preschool and kindergarten teachers must be included in curriculum development so that identified outcomes for children reflect sound child development and practice.

If you are working in a community where all of this is happening, then your work will be made easy, and children will benefit greatly. If you are working in a community where little of this is happening, we hope you will round up a group of respected colleagues to become more vocal about what is needed for young children's optimal education, and that you will not stop in your efforts until you accomplish what is needed. When communities look at outcomes for their children on state tests, which usually begin at grade four, and expect that educational oversight and support is not very important in the early years, they will never obtain what they want or what children need.

Sometimes, unintended educational deficits in the earliest years go unrecognized in communities and cannot be remediated later, despite good intentions or regrets. Certainly, this creates challenges in communities as children grow to adulthood, unprepared to contribute to a strong workforce or community vitality in any meaningful way.

However, the oversight is even more serious in terms of human development. Whether a child has ample opportunity to reach optimal potential should not be left to chance, and adults who can provide for a rich and promising beginning for children in their communities should make every effort to do so.

Chapter 3

Emerging Literacy Components and Teaching Strategies

B ecause our goal is to increase children's oral language, writing, and reading concepts and skills during the year we have them in our classrooms, we must keep two ideas solidly in the forefront of

[I]t is vital to ensure that preschoolers and kindergartners gain control of foundational skills in developmentally appropriate ways. First and second grades are filled with children who lack this foundation and who, as a result, have difficulty trying to build key reading skills as the tasks become increasingly difficult.

EHRI & ROBERTS, 2006

our daily teaching: Children must have very good adult models to develop these skills, and they must have a chance to practice what they see to become more proficient.

Teachers have responded well to the task of designing engaging research-based activities, but many tell us that there just isn't enough time in the day to get it all done—or done well—and frustration levels are high. We must become better guardians of children's time and become more vocal

about the many distractions that get in the way of good teaching. When the "specials" and other curricular demands crowd out any chance of solid blocks of time to focus on literacy, or we have to move good instruction around to fit in all the "extras," chances are that development during the year will not be optimal. It simply can't be.

Therefore, the first line of attack in establishing a quality literacy program is to make sure that there is an uninterrupted block of time, at least one hour each morning, devoted to involving children in a balanced, creative presentation of literacy activities. This is not to say that we don't need music, art, and physical activity in early childhood classrooms. They are essential, as are the specialists who have expertise in these areas. However, rather than wasting children's valuable time by herding them down hallways to receive instruction, we would like to have the specialists work with classroom teachers to integrate high-quality music, visual art, dramatics, movement and dance, and other physical activity into the ongoing program during the day. McDonald and Fisher (2006, 2) contend that "simply put, learning with and through the arts enlivens instruction, increases student involvement, and deepens both the meaning and memory of the learning at hand," particularly as related to literacy skills. Involvement in the arts is one of the characteristics of the Reggio Emilia programs that make them so attractive to children, families, and early childhood professionals. Such an approach would call for a change in the way we do business in a lot of programs, but many centers and schools have done so in the best interest of children.

Many early childhood programs are becoming all-day programs, with a focus on early literacy for at least half a day. Others are concentrating more literacy activity into half-day programs. We'd like to suggest a half-day schedule (Figure 3.1) that offers large- and small-group activities and opportunities for teachers to work individually with children. You can tweak this a bit, depending on your own program, but you will need to include a group meeting during which you can demonstrate literacy activity and at least one hour for carefully constructed center activity. There should be as few transitions and wasted time as possible. You'll notice that we've included outdoor time, which has suffered in many programs because of the academic focus that dominates the schedule. You'll notice, too, that we put outdoor time at the end, having had experience with dressing and undressing children for cold weather, which can take all morning itself! We do have time to

Time Allocated	Type of Activity
15 minutes	Arrival, sign in, and use of designated center materials by children while waiting for group time to begin; Greeting each child and conversing briefly with individual and small groups of children by teacher
20 minutes	Whole-group morning gathering, morning messages, predictable chart, write-alouds, sharing the pen, concept charts, modeling of center-based activity
60 minutes	Activity time in literacy-enriched play settings, including drawing/writing activity; teacher working with individual and small groups of children on literacy activities suited to their needs; mini skill-building workshops centered on word skills offered during this time; brief, individual assessments also completed
20 minutes	Clean-up and snack
15 minutes	Shared storybook reading, echo reading, big books, guest readers, mystery readers, story webs
35 minutes	Active literacy experiences: finger plays, poems, reader's theater, music and movement; letter/object find races; walking the room and school to read print; puppet play, word games
10 minutes	Review of the day and preparation for going home
20 minutes	Outdoor play, with inclusion of literacy movement games, jump rope chants; teacher saying goodbye to each child

FIGURE **3.1**

Sample Half-Day
Schedule

get in what children need, and a session like this every day would allow for plenty of literacy concept and skill building. We're not a big fan of having children spend time in lining up to make transitions, but believe these should happen more naturally. Don't spend large amounts of time waiting for children to arrive at a large group. Get started with an exciting opener each time so that children *want* to be there to participate and not miss the fun. So that children can learn routines, we'd stick pretty closely to this type of schedule every day, but if we found we needed to adapt it because children got intensely interested in something, it would be perfectly okay to do so. Having different genres of music playing when children enter the classroom is a good idea, and a teacher who looks happy to begin the day is always terrific!

Expanding to a full-day schedule (Figure 3.2) doesn't mean stuffing literacy into a half day, of course, because there are many opportunities to integrate literacy throughout the entire day.

Use the times that children are active and up and about the room to do the same yourself. This is wonderful observation and interaction time, and your clipboard and/or sticky notes should be handy so that you can make notations about individual children as you talk with them about their interests and what they are learning about literacy.

Components and Strategies

One of the things we've tried to make clear in this text is that we have to begin to simplify our approach to literacy teaching during this earliest period. In this chapter we suggest some activities to which children respond very well and we divided it into three major sections:

1. Oral language development (including listening, receptive and expressive language, and vocabulary), phonological awareness, and phonemic awareness

2. Early writing, including developmental stages, letter–grapheme association, and understanding of the alphabetic principle

3. Early reading, including sight word recognition, beginning decoding skills, story element recognition, and comprehension

Time Allocated	Type of Activity
30 minutes	Arrival, sign in, teacher greeting children, limited activity/materials choice, lunch count
20 minutes	Morning meeting (whole-group gathering), morning message, predictable chart, write-alouds, sharing the pen, concept charts, modeling and explanation of literacy rotation activity
50 minutes	Literacy rotations (children rotate every 15 minutes to one of three planned centers: teacher mini lesson, writing, independent/partner reading)
15 minutes	Clean-up, washing hands, snack
20 minutes	Music and movement, reader's theater
60 minutes	Self-selected activity in a print-rich environment with activity options heavily directed toward acquisition of literacy and language skills
15 minutes	Clean-up, washing hands
45 minutes	Lunch
15 minutes	Return to group, shared storybook reading
15 minutes	Afternoon group meeting (modeling and explanation of math/science center activity available)
45 minutes	Math, science rotations with integrated literacy skill building
30 minutes	Clean-up and review of the day, daily message
30 minutes	Preparation for going home, outdoor play and dismissal

FIGURE **3.2**

Sample Full-Day
Schedule

A brief introduction to each of these foci is provided and followed by principles for general application in the classroom. Samples of activities to support children's development are also included.

Because activities are richer if they combine elements to build oral language, reading, and writing concepts and skills, the activities presented often cross into more than one area. Always begin the year with activities that involve print or vocabulary most familiar to children; their names and logographic print (names they see frequently in the environment such as Burger King, Cheerios, Exit, Stop; Figure 3.3) are at the top of the list. As children begin to be familiar with other children's names and a few sight words, these can also be used before expanding to more sophisticated activities.

In your daily lessons, be sure to design a balance of in-depth activities that address all areas of literacy development. Literacy activities just seem to flow out of creative teachers, and children in rooms where teachers use engaging activities rather than ditto sheets are the lucky

FIGURE **3.3**

Environmental
Print Wall

children, because their understanding of print is so much more in depth and usable as they progress from level to level. The activities we've included here may be familiar ones to you. All are tried and tested with real children and teachers who found them highly appealing. You may think of many ways to adapt these and create still others.

Oral Language, and Phonological and Phonemic Awareness Development

The oral language component is probably the most ignored in terms of conscious, active planning by teachers. Yet, it is the one that will underscore (or hamper) a child's later ability to be an effective speaker, listener, reader, and writer.

Children learn to speak quite naturally; this is an expected development, built into the human species (Bruer, 1999). However, the quality of their language (breadth of vocabulary, grammar, syntax) is heavily dependent on the models they have and what happens during those interactions.

The young child's phonological awareness is an aspect that develops during preschool years. Key skills children need to develop phonological awareness necessary for reading and spelling include rhyming, blending onsets and rimes, noting beginning sounds, and segmenting sounds in words (Gunning, 2000, 2). Children will not pick up these skills without being given targeted experiences, and we cannot expect that all entering kindergarten children have had them. We may need to provide extended periods of time and instruction for them to develop these skills, but in the interest of their ability to become solid readers and spellers later on, we will want to make sure we don't hurry them past this period before the skills can be documented.

According to Marcia Invernizzi (2003, 144–145), phonological awareness is a "broad construct that encompasses linguistic features as expansive as the syncopation of stress across syllables (IN-ver-NIZ-zi) or as contained as syllables within words. It also refers to sound features within syllables like **alliteration,** rhyme, and individual phonemes." She goes on to say that children become confused when they are asked to identify various speech sounds; they can hear them, but they may not understand what a teacher wants when asking the child to refer to the "first sound" or location of sounds in a segmented word. She recommends having children tap to the rhythm of nursery rhymes to achieve the one-to-one correspondence between stressed syllables and meaningful words in the rhymes (e.g., JACK and JILL went UP the HILL). This leads to an understanding of stressed syllables as a segue to the "most important concept of all—beginning sounds."

Phonemic awareness is tougher and takes longer to develop. This calls for the understanding that words are made up of a number of sounds or phonemes, the ability to blend and segment words, and the ability to manipulate sounds to form different words. Child development plays an enormously important part in this, calling for a child to handle two aspects of language at once, putting aside the content of the language to pay attention to its form. An important task for the young child is to learn the 26 capital and lowercase letter shapes and to associate them with the letter names and phonemes. When we eliminate the 12 lowercase shapes that match their capitals (e.g., c, k, o), beginners must learn 40 distinctive shapes. Many five- and six-year-olds will not yet have developed the decentralization, and perhaps fluid neural development, to be able to deal with this adequately, and you can see how there can be confusion about sets of letters such as b-d-p-q-g, h-n-r, m-w, uy—x, s-z, i-j, and L-I, l, I (Ehri & Roberts, 2006, 13; Gunning, 2002; Harris & Sipay, 1990).

Young children are highly influenced by adults in their world, and there are some proven strategies that adults can use to help children become proficient language users, as well as to develop an underlying conceptual framework for phonological and phonemic awareness:

1. Model appropriate language structure—namely, complete sentences, correct grammar, tone of voice, volume, and speed. Without creating stilted communication, encourage children to use complete sentences in their responses to you and to each other. This is especially important for the child who has underdeveloped language. In a friendly way, reinforce the rules of good listening and speaking.

2. Respond to children's language by restating what they say (particularly if there is incorrect grammar or sentence structure) without

actively calling attention to their mistakes. Expand on their statements, using new words and elaboration to build vocabulary and understanding of syntax, and to clarify meaning. Ask open-ended questions and then let children take the conversational lead.

3. Use language in playful ways (e.g., rhyming, substituting initial sounds, singing, chanting), helping children develop the phonological awareness that will later support their learning to read. Recite songs, nursery rhymes, and poems together; have telephones in the room that can be used for conversation. Imagine things aloud. Tell stories instead of always reading them. Encourage children to make up stories and retell familiar stories. Play games that focus on intent listening and word games that use their names: "What if all of your names started with G and the sound guh? How would Hessen's name sound? Karen's name?" Select books that reinforce alliteration and rhyming. Use songs and song charts to promote vocabulary, rhythm, concepts of print, and a sense of story elements and sequence (e.g., *Going on a Bear Hunt*, *There Was an Old Lady Who Swallowed a Fly*, *Wheels on the Bus*, and *Down by the Bay*) (McDonald & Fisher, 2006). Help children create new words to a familiar tune such as "Twinkle, Twinkle, Little Star," or new endings to an existing, familiar poem. With help, even very young children can do this, and you'll be surprised at how much they enjoy making up their own rhymes, songs, and finger plays.

4. Allow children plenty of time for meaningful, polite conversation with peers and with you to express their ideas, to talk through problems, to imagine or fantasize out loud, and to ask questions. Greet and have a brief conversation with each child. Talk about the day at the end of the day. Share your feelings, likes, and dislikes, and encourage the children to do the same. Explain a game. Talk about sensitive issues as they occur. Discuss reasons for things. When reading aloud to them, encourage them to predict what will happen and to talk about connections between what's happening in the story and their own experiences.

Use snack time and mealtime for conversation, rather than just a time to refuel.

5. Structure opportunities for more formal "presentations" by children, such as small-group or one-on-one show-and-tell (it's even hard for the teacher to sit through everyone having a turn presenting to the large group), reader's theater, author's chair (when children read something they've written and then respond to questions), and artist's talk (when children tell a story about a picture they've drawn).

6. Encourage friendship building. Silent, isolated children are not building language facility. Model verbal problem-solving strategies and expect children to use them during conflict situations. Give scripts to children who are not skilled in negotiating social interaction with others: "If you want to play, Kara, maybe you could ask, 'Can I be the truck driver who brings the bread?'" "When Deondre grabs materials from you, Tara, tell him, 'I don't like it when you grab things because I'm using them. Instead of grabbing, ask me if we can share.'" Cooperative learning activities and activities such as block building, open-ended art activities, and dramatic play support the development of communication skills.

7. Include activities in which children hear, say, and see language simultaneously. This helps children at all stages to see some of the connections between oral and written language, and to build phonological awareness (Kostelnik et al., 2004). Having song charts, finger plays, and favorite poems available for children to view and follow while participating is a favorite, and if they're kept out and available in the room, you may often see a couple of children using them during open sessions or even writing their own versions (Figure 3.4).

8. Concentrate daily on providing activities that teach the following concepts and skills: rhyme, phonemic awareness, **segmentation**, sound substitution, active listening, story retelling, effective oral language skills, speaking and listening for a variety of purposes, ways to formulate questions and answers, and ways to give and follow directions.

9. Read good, rich literature every day to enhance vocabulary and familiarize children with the more complex use of oral language. Keep in mind that books that are highly decodable, with controlled vocabulary, have a place in literacy learning. We want to underscore, however, that the purpose in using these books is to help children unlock the reading code, not to build vocabulary, thus the reason for including another type of literature every day.

10. Provide activities that help children develop effective and differentiated listening skills, such as the following (Soderman et al., 2005, 114):

- Use rhythm sticks or hands to tap or clap out the syllable patterns in words and names.

- Go on sound walks to discover sounds in the environment.

- Play games such as Simon Says and games such as charades to emphasize nonverbal "listening."

- Play tapes of sounds they can identify, or help children make their own tapes.

- Ask questions prior to the reading of a story, pointing out vocabulary words or concepts for which they need to listen.

- Play sound discrimination games.

FIGURE **3.4**

My Name Is
Stegasaurus

- Play games such as Guess What's in the Bag? Guess What's in My Hand? Guess What I'm Thinking About?, in which they have to listen to clues until they guess correctly.

- Have them respond to multistep directions or repeat in correct sequence and detail a message they hear.

- Provide plenty of rhyming activities and written examples of rhyme.

- Model good listening behaviors and discuss useful listening strategies, such as looking directly at someone who is speaking, sitting relatively still, and waiting for one's turn to speak.

11. Teach children the many, many functions of talk outlined by Michael Halliday (1975): that language can be used to satisfy needs (instrumental), to control the behavior of others (regulatory), to get along with others (interactional), to tell about one's self (personal), to learn about things (heuristic), to pretend or make believe (imaginative), and to inform others (informative). Give them scripts they need when they don't seem to understand that words can be more powerful than hitting, yelling, or biting.

12. Discuss with parents their important role in developing children's vocabularies and language by reading, having discussions about what the *child* is interested in talking about, and by modeling good sentence use. Tell parents about some of the observations of Hart and Risley (2003) in the study they did to identify meaningful differences in the everyday experiences of American children.

Suggested Activities to Enhance Oral Language Development, and Phonological and Phonemic Awareness

Silly Names. Tell the children, "If Reynard's name started with a B, it would be Beynard. That would be silly, wouldn't it? Let's be silly. Let's say all our names as if they all started with a B."

Morning Meeting. Hold a morning meeting each day, and begin it with friendship-building strategies. Start with their names. After reading *Brown Bear, Brown Bear*, give a beanbag to a child (in this case, named Jason) and have children say, "Jason, Jason, who do you see?" He could then say, "I see Ashley looking at me." He would then toss the bag to her and the group would continue with, "Ashley, Ashley, who do you see?" Another activity is to sing their names: "Tell me your name." Child sings back, "My name is Jason," and then turns to another child, singing, "Tell me your name." Continue around the circle, including the teacher.

Auditory Memory Games.   Build children's auditory memory and listening skills by having them repeat in correct detail and sequence a message they hear. Seat children in a circle (use a small group at first so they have less to remember). Begin the process by saying, "I'm going to the grocery store this morning and I'm planning to buy some carrots." The child to your right repeats, "I'm going to the grocery store this morning, and I'm planning to buy some carrots and _____" (child adds an item). Continue around the circle. Be sure to eliminate competitive aspects of the game. If a child can't remember the articles in sequence, have the group help him or her. Go on only as long as the children seem to be enjoying the challenge of remembering the number of items. Repeat this kind of activity by going on a trip and packing a suitcase with _____, by going to the zoo to see _____, a farm to hear _____, and so on.

Hink Pinks.   Hink Pinks (Cunningham, 2000) are rhyming pairs. After children have the concept of rhyme, play a game with them by giving them a first word and having them give you back a rhyme (e.g., fake/snake, cold/gold, hen/pen, duck/truck, rag/bag) if they can think of one. Children catch on very quickly to this and it helps them enormously in their later reading and writing.

Telephone Talk.   Provide a set of telephones and message pads. Encourage children to call each other and to practice telling and writing messages, to make the connection between spoken and written language.

Nursery Rhyme Dismissal.   Explain to the children that you will tell the first part of a nursery rhyme and a child can give the last part to be excused from a large group. Choose the most familiar rhyme for the children who may have the least experience with them and only begin this process when all children have had some experience in the classroom with nursery rhymes.

Letter Sound Race.   Select a letter and talk about the sound it makes (e.g., p, puh). Show the children a few objects that start with that letter (e.g., pencil, pen, paper). Tell the children, "We're going to get into two teams and see how many things in the room we can find together in five minutes that start with the 'puh' sound." At the end of five minutes, count the number of objects and have the children say the name of the object, emphasizing the beginning sound.

Phonogram Fun.   One of the secrets of early reading is discovering the concept of onsets and rimes—when you can change the beginning of words and make a completely new word, lots of them. It's good to talk with children about the fact that these are "families" of words. You can illustrate this by showing children the "am" family and how putting a P on the beginning turns the word into *Pam.* "What other words can be made if we erase the P and put another beginning letter (Sam, bam, ram, jam, ham, dam, ram, and so on)?" Children can experiment with other "families" (there are 37 in all, with the most familiar being ill, ake, it, uck, an, in, ell, at). Phonogram wheels can be made with a cut-out section on the first wheel on which the rime is written and the back shows a different onset each time it is spun. The wheels can be held together with a grommet in the middle. Flip charts can also be made, with the longest one in the back containing the rime and onsets stapled on the front that, when flipped, will reveal a different word each time. Children should be encouraged to write down the word family they are exploring with these tools, perhaps in their journals. Family members can make these tools in an evening make-it-and-take-it session and take them home for children to practice reading.

Finger Play Role Play.   Have children take part in standing during a finger play and taking on the role of one of the characters. A stick puppet can be added, with the words from that line printed on the back. For example, Lynne Munson had her children participating in the finger play "Five Little Pumpkins" as follows:

Everyone:	Five little pumpkins sitting on a gate.
	The first one said,
Child 1:	"My, it's getting late!"
Everyone:	The second one said,
Child 2:	"There are witches in the air!"
Everyone:	The third one said,
Child 3:	"But we don't care!"
Everyone:	The fourth one said,
Child 4:	"Let's run and run and run!"
Everyone:	The fifth one said,
Child 5:	"I'm ready for some fun!"
Everyone:	Ooooooo went the wind and
	Out went the lights [clap hands]!
	The five little pumpkins rolled out of sight!

Song to Dismiss from Large Group (Tune: "Frére Jacques")

I am thinking . . .
I am thinking . . .
Where I'll go, where I'll go.
I am thinking . . .
I am thinking . . .
What I'll do, what I'll do.

Song to Signal Clean Up (Tune: "Mary Had a Little Lamb")

It's time to put our things away
  Things away
  Things away
It's time to put our things away
  And sit right down!

Song to Collect Materials Used in a Large Group (Tune: "Row, Row, Row Your Boat")

> Pass, pass, pass the books
>
> Pass the books to me
>
> Pass, pass, pass the books
>
> Pass them right to me!

Song to Bring Children to a Large Group (Tune: "Pop Goes the Weasel")

> *First verse:*
>
> All around the classroom
>
> The children hide in boxes (have children scrunch down, wherever they are when they hear you sing this)
>
> Where they are, nobody knows
>
> Pop go the children!

> *Second verse:*
>
> All around the classroom
>
> The children come to large group.
>
> They find their place right on the rug
>
> Ready to listen!

Itsy Bitsy Spider Group Sing. Supply foot-square pieces of tagboard on which the children paint a spider on one side and a sun on the other side. During a large-group session, have the children stand to sing "Itsy Bitsy Spider," holding up the side showing the spider and alternating to the side, showing the sun as appropriate.

Bag Story. Prepare to tell a familiar story or fable to the children that involves only two to three characters. Inside a paper bag, place simple stick puppets to represent the characters. Say to the children, "I want you to listen very carefully. I am going to tell you a story. The story is in this bag. When I'm finished, I'll give you a bag with the same puppets in it and you can work with another person to tell the story. Then, when you go home today, each of you can take a bag of puppets home so that you can tell the story with someone at home. Look up here and listen to my story."

Letter Name and Sound Dismissal. Dismiss children from a large group by saying, "I'm going to say a letter and the sound it makes. If your first name begins with that letter and that sound, stand up and spell your whole name before you leave for snack. If your name has the letter R in it and the sound 'arrr,' stand up and spell your name."

Big Word, Small Word Sort. Tell the children you have to sort some words and need their help. Some of the words have only one syllable, some have two, and some have three or more. Have a pocket chart, labeled with "one syllable, two syllables," "three syllables" or more. Remind the children that they have clapped syllables to one another's names, and model that with John, Kaelin, and Dequarius, putting the names under the correct titles. Then hold up a number of individual cards on which are printed words with varying syllables, say the word, have the children clap the syllables, and then have them tell you in which column you should put the word. After children have done this a number of times in large or small group, the activity may be placed in the language arts area for individuals or pairs of children to use.

Name Comparisons. List all the children's names on an easel. Compare two names (the shortest and the longest) and have children guess which is longest and which is shortest. Count the number of letters. Move to two other names, increasing the difficulty. For example, ask, "Does Ryan have any of the same letters as Mary?" Point out the first letters. Ask, "Why are all the first letters different?" "Are there any names that rhyme with lots of words (e.g., Mike)?" Clap the syllables. Ask, "How many beats (or syllables) in Jasmine's name?" "How many of the names begin with the same letter?" "Is there one name that begins with a letter no one else's name begins with (usually Q)?" "How many of the names end in 'e'?" "Can we hear that 'e' when we say those names? Let's say the names."

Literacy Action Play. Turn children's favorite familiar books into action play. For example, provide children with three three-sided boards to paint, turning them into each of the three little pigs' houses. Act out the story of the three little pigs, having children act as either one of the pigs or a group of them acting as the wolf, blowing down the first two houses but having trouble with the third, which is made of bricks. Stories they love to act out are *The Three Billy Goats Gruff, Jack and the Bean Stalk, Goldilocks and the Three Bears,* and lots of others. The addition of the cardboard props, which they have painted themselves, just adds to the fun.

Early Writing Development

As soon as children discover that what we think about can be saved by writing it down for others to see, development follows fairly swiftly if frequent opportunity and modeling are provided. Writing, as you know, begins with the scribble stage, during which the child makes undifferentiated marks because they see adults and older peers doing something like that. Children then move to making marks that look like letters and put random letters together, often copying them from the environment (prephonemic stage). After they move into the semi-phonemic stage, we see them using some letters to stand for sounds they hear in words, but not every sound (phoneme) will be represented. During the fourth stage, the phonemic stage, we can see their awareness of phonemes, and they can sometimes be seen grinding out the sounds, making sure there is a letter for each sound they think of, usually only consonants. Vowels then begin to make their appearance, and sometimes children will overcompensate at this stage, throwing in a few more vowels than are needed, but being very proud that they can demonstrate this knowledge. During the transitional stage, we begin to see standard spelling of words, and there is a mixed bag—a combination of writing sounds for each phoneme and conventionally spelled words. Finally, during the sixth stage (standard spelling), "adult" or dictionary spelling has become the norm for the child and we see most words spelled correctly. That's what we're aiming for!

Scaffolded writing sessions have proved helpful in creating a visual model for young children about how to put separate words together to form a sentence. Work with individual children to plan a message by drawing separate lines for each word the child says, matching the length of the word to the approximate length of the line. Then ask the child to reflect the message, while you point to each of the lines. Afterward, ask the child to attempt to write each of the words in the spaces provided, using any letters he or she know that would represent the sounds in each word. In the use of this strategy, you are an obvious resource, but the lines also provide assistance as a placeholder in helping the child remember the sequence and length of the message, as well as something about the length of the word (Bodrova & Leong, 2001, 2003, 2006).

Going beyond the spelling of words and writing initial sentences, children will learn a great deal more about what constitutes a good piece of writing. Although very young children may not yet have developed the traits of a good writer, they will benefit by having you model the following characteristics and talk about them as you write for them (McDonald & Fisher, 2006, 11):

1. Ideas, the heart of the message

2. Organization, the internal structure of the piece

3. Voice, the personal tone and flavor of the author's message

4. Word choice, the vocabulary a writer chooses to convey meaning

5. Sentence fluency, the rhythm and flow of the language

6. Conventions, the mechanical correctness

7. Presentation, how the writing actually looks on the page

This happens best through brief modeling of writing on a daily basis, using such activities as morning message, daily news, predictable charts, thank-you notes after a field trip or having a visitor, and writing for real purposes. Use every opportunity to involve children in saving their ideas and sharing them with others by using print.

Rubin and Carlan (2005) suggest that analyzing bilingual children's writing is the best way for us to understand what the children understand about the relationship between their two developing languages. All children, regardless of whether they are bilingual, need to be doing a lot of writing every day and to see the teacher write every day so they can begin to value how powerful writing is in our everyday lives. Children's writing should be displayed liberally about the classroom and valued, no matter which of the previous stages the child is in. There has been a difference of opinion about this, with some educators and parents wanting only to display "mechanically correct" pieces of writing. If this is the case, please develop and convey a rationale about why it's important to celebrate the different stages and evidence of development. Children are proud of their work, and we need to be also. Watching us daily as we model writing and seeing lots of print in other places, including the books we read for them, they will move through the stages they need to in order to become good spellers and writers. As they begin to write numbers of words and become highly familiar with the alphabet, they will begin to use a large-print dictionary when they are uncertain about how to spell a word. This, however, should not be expected of preschool and kindergarten children. They have their own age-expected developmental tasks and, if we do our jobs well, they will discover quite a lot about writing and all its uses in the time they spend with us.

Some general ideas that should be observed when we purposefully plan for writing instruction are the following:

1. Use children's names as an introduction to writing (see suggested activities later). Have them sign in every day and sign their name to all work. One of our teachers uses this activity as a way to teach vocabulary as well. She will often supply two sign-in lists. On the top of each one, she places a different object or animal. On this particular morning she has a picture of a cuscus (a tree-dwelling marsupial from Australia that has foxlike ears and a prehensile tail) and a jackal. She asks the children, "Would you rather sign in on the cuscus' list or the jackal's?" Sometimes, she will take characters out of familiar books they have read. Other times, she will select two different flowers (a daffodil and a Shasta daisy), or an uppercase and a lowercase A, or two different letters, or two different wall words—anything to focus their attention.

2. Place writing materials in *every* center and encourage children to integrate writing into their play, even if it's "pretend" writing. Be thoughtful about this. Explain to the children what the

materials are all about and why you have placed them there. Just putting them into the center may not be enough, and they may go unnoticed or unused without some explanation and suggested use.

3. Model writing every day for different purposes (morning message; daily news; a class book; a predictable chart; attribute naming; a thank-you note on the easel; a familiar nursery rhyme, song, finger play, or poem).

4. Encourage children to draw and write for many purposes, and plan to have them write every day. Have them learn to date all their work for comparison purposes so that they and their family members can track skill development. Do not write in children's journals. This is not a place for them to dictate to you. The journals are for their writing only. If they want to dictate to you, write what they say, exactly as they say it, on a separate piece of paper, and allow them to copy it. After they have the concept of letter–sound association and can write letters, do not let them dictate to you any longer. Do not give children sentences you have made up to copy in their journals. Do not allow children to have others write words for them in their journals. If they want to have another child help them spell a word, have the helping child write it on a separate piece of paper. Encourage children to use resources such as the word wall, concept charts in the classroom, and their heads to think about words. Help them to learn about stretching words out so that individual sounds can be matched to letters they can write. Do not allow them to become reliant on you or another child for the thinking they must do to break through into independent writing. Finally, do not (under any circumstances)

correct a child's journal entry. During the emergent literacy stage, this would actually be a deterrent to the child's development.

5. Teach letter–sound association in as many ways as you can, taking advantage of many activities such as those listed here. Make sure to do this on a daily basis.

6. Plan activities that get across the following concepts and skills:

Writing and pictures convey meaning, thoughts, and ideas.

Letters are formed in a specific way and are unchanging (alphabetic principle).

Letters stand for sounds in language.

There are twenty-six letters that can be combined in different ways.

Anything that is said can be written down.

Print says the same thing today as it will say tomorrow.

Writing is arranged in a line; a picture or a graphic is arranged differently.

Words are what you read; pictures can help us understand text, but you do not read pictures.

7. Help children connect their writing to other areas of the curriculum. For example, Sue Edland, Lansing kindergarten teacher, often brings in interesting science material for children to observe and then to write about their discoveries in their journals (Figure 3.5).

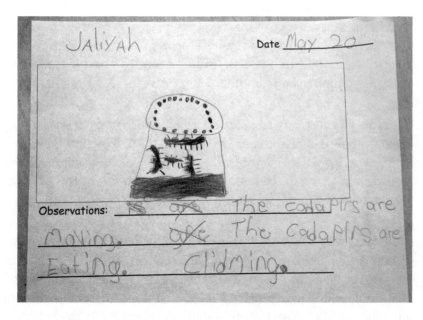

Emerging Literacy Components and Teaching Strategies

FIGURE **3.5**

After observing the caterpiller Jaliyah writes, "The caterpillars are moving. The caterpillars are eating. Climbing."

Suggested Activities to Enhance Early Writing Ability, Letter-Sound and Letter-Grapheme Association, and Understanding of Alphabetic Principle

Fingerpaint/Sand Tray Names. Supply sand trays or trays filled with fingerpaints. Have children practice writing their names or the names of classmates or other words they know. See what happens to the name when a piece of paper is placed on the fingerpaint, capturing the name. Does it look the same?

Secret Name. Have a secret name on the easel, with only the initial letter written in, and have children write underneath what they believe the name is (and sign their name after their guess).

Magna Doodles and Mini Whiteboards. Supply individual draw-and-erase boards that can be used by children alone or in small or large groups, as you model particular letters or words to write. These can be

purchased at a number of office supply places, variety stores, or commercial groups such as Lakeshore Learning (www.lakeshorelearning.com). Children can copy and then quickly erase as you move on to another letter or word.

Message Center.   Establish a board on which you have tacks that children can easily handle. Have children make a picture for a friend and any writing they can do, fold it up, put the child's name on the outside, and pin it to the message board. For children who never get a message, make up one and have the child write back to you.

Name Cut-up.   Provide children with envelopes in which you have cut up the letters of their name and have them reconstruct their name. This can also be done using a pocket chart. Place the separated letters of a child's name in the top row. Have the child reassemble the letters in a number of different ways, spelling a new word in the bottom row. They can write each word in their journals before going on to the next word. Two children can work together on this by combining their names.

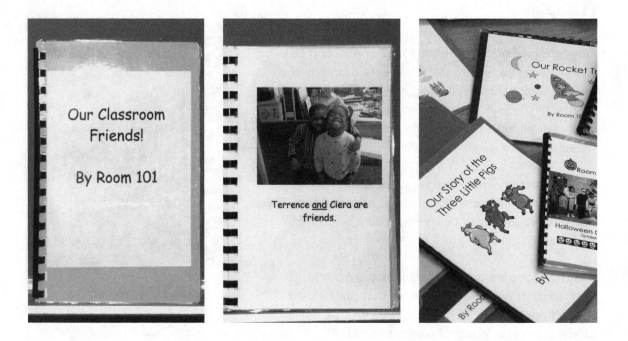

Terrence _and_ Ciera are
friends.

Word Write.   Give the children a set of **movable letters** (at first, just the letters in their name) and see if they can discover "little words" they can make from the letters, which they then write in their journal. Have them work with another child to put the letters from both their names together to see what words they can come up with.

Book Making.   There are all kinds of books children can make (pop-up, peek-a-boo, shape, content, and class books). A book about you, complete with pictures and brief written descriptions on each page, is a wonderful first introduction. It can be followed with a "friends book," a class book in which each page has a photo of a child in the class and the child's name clearly written on the bottom of the page. Another example of a class book is to make a "Clifford's Birthday Book." Have each child draw a self-portrait on a page on which you print at the bottom, "Hi, I am _____." (a line on which the child prints his or her name). On the next page, have the child draw a picture of something he would like to give Clifford for a present. On the bottom of the page, write, "I gave Clifford _____ (a line on which the child prints what he gave Clifford). You can also print, "He liked my present best!" and put all these produced pages together into a class book that the children can use to reread familiar phrases. (You can use these as a familiar book to read during the morning meetings to encourage children's ability to read them independently.) Class books can be put together on a regular basis and placed in the reading center, where children love to read and reread them.

Sometimes, it's fun to rewrite a real book, changing what the author has written. Erica Poindexter, one of our laboratory teachers, has had children take the text from Karen Berman Nagel's *Our Silly Garden*, rewriting the text: "Today, we took some [the children chose the word *pencils*]. We put them in the ground. We sprinkled them with [they chose *salt*] . . . and smiled at what we found: [*erasers*] next to the carrots and [*journals*] among the peas . . . . Order this book if you don't have it and see what great fun you can have rewriting the text and then starting all over again with completely different words. The children look forward to recreating and come up with some silly scenarios. They also learn how sentences are formed and how certain words can be substituted for others when writing.

Predictable Charts. On the easel, announce a title for the predictable chart for that day (e.g., Our Favorite Thing to Play With) and then write a sentence for each child in which all the words in the sentences are exactly the same (predictable), except for the child's name and the thing the child names. For example:

> **Carrie's favorite toy is a bike.**
> **Renita's favorite toy is Barbie.**
> **Kevin's favorite toy is Legos.**

> or

> **My favorite toy is a bike. (Carrie)**
> **My favorite toy is a Barbie. (Renita)**
> **My favorite toy is a Legos set. (Kevin)**

After everyone has had a chance to name something, have the class read each of the sentences and observe any similarities they see (e.g., every sentence starts with someone's name, there is a period after each sentence, all the names start with an uppercase or capital letter, the longest word is *favorite,* the shortest word is *a*). When a predictable chart is complete, a class book can be made from it. Cut the sentences into strips and give each one to the child who dictated it. The child can then illustrate the sentence. All the pages can be put together into a class book that the children can reread. As an additional activity, cut each sentence into a strip and then cut each strip into separate words for the child to reassemble, paste, and illustrate.

Whiteboard Write. Challenge a pair of children to work together at a whiteboard to write as many letters or words as they can.

Journal Writing.   Have children get into the habit of writing in their journals every day. After they have been making pictures for a while and signing their names, move them into writing something about the picture by having them draw a line across the page in the middle of the paper. The upper half will be for the picture and the lower half will be for their writing about the picture. If they cannot yet make an association between the sound they want and the letter, have them dictate to you. However, after they begin to make letter–sound associations, have them attempt the writing and accept what they put down, rereading it with them.

Morning Message/Daily News.   Each day, model writing by doing the morning message or daily news activity. Select a child to give you a message to write down (or something that happened during the day or something he or she learned to do that day). On an easel pad used just for morning message or daily news, write the date each time and have the children help you spell the words to put down. Have the children read the sentence afterward. You can begin the message with the name of the person who gave the message, putting what they said in quotation marks: Jasmine said, "My mom had a new baby. She's at the hospital." Talk to the children about quotation marks or "talking marks" (be sure to use the real name) and what they mean. Children like these and begin to catch on to using them very early. Leave all the messages for the entire week together. On Tuesday, read Monday's message prior to beginning the writing of Tuesday's. Each day, read all the messages up to that point prior to writing the new message. If writing more than one sentence, always reread the sentences written up to that point before writing a new sentence.

Message Fill-in.   On the easel, prepare a sheet for morning meeting with a message to the children, but omit letters from words they are likely to be able to sound out. For example:

G_ _d _orning. Today _ _ Friday. _oday, t_ e date is _ay 23, 2003.

To_ay, the weather is _____.

Word Wall and Walk/Write the Room.   Place your word wall by your writing center so that children can refer to it. It should be at the children's eye level. Begin the year's word wall by putting children's names up, one day at a time. Draw a child's name from a box. Tell the children, for example, "This word is Jamel's name. It takes letters to write his name. Each of the letters in Jamel's name have their own names." Say each letter. Have the children chant the letters with you. Count the letters. Point out that Jamel begins with the letter J and that it looks bigger than the other letters because it is an uppercase (or capital) letter and all the other letters are lowercase. Cut up the name in front of the children and place the letters in a pocket chart out of order. Ask Jamel if he can put them in the right order. As he does, have the children say the letters. On another card, print Jamel's name and place it on the word wall under J. Incorporate other sight words on the word wall and encourage children to use the words in their writing attempts. Each day, walk the room, reading as much print as possible, including the words on the word wall. Children can also "write the room" by taking a clipboard around the room (or, accompanied by an adult, around the school or neighborhood) to write down any words they see.

Curved or Straight? Use a pocket chart for this activity to teach children the straight or curved characteristics of upper- and lowercase letters. Make three categories: "Straight," "Curved," and "Straight and Curved." Present letters to children on cards (e.g., A, B, C, D). Ask, "Are there just straight lines to make this letter, only curved lines, or straight and curved?" Say, "Watch me make this letter" [talking it through]. Have a child come up and place the letter in the right category or column.

Wormy Letters. Cut up large, thick rubber bands and make "worms" out of them. Have the children form different letters with the worms, seeing which letters can be formed out of straight worms, which can be formed out of curvy worms, and which letters need both curvy and straight worms. Have them record all the different wormy letters they were able to make by writing them on a small whiteboard that's been placed on the table near the "worms."

Who's Not Here? As a way of demon- strating the spelling of children's names, ask "Who's not here this morning? Which of our friends is missing?" As children tell you who's missing, list their names. For example,

1. Eddie
2. Javon
3. Zhane

Ask children to help with the sound and letter to start the name. As they become more familiar with writing one another's name, you will want to share the pen with the children and have someone come forward to help with the writing of the names.

Name Gift. At the beginning of the year, fill small baggies with lami- nated letters to make up each child's name. Tie the bag with colorful ribbon and tell the child, "I have a gift for you. It's the letters of your name. We're going to practice this activity here today, and then you can take this home and show someone that you know how to form the letters in your name." Have letters available and cards that have the children's individual names printed. Have the children match the let- ters to the letters on the card. Have them scramble the letters and do it again. This activity can be used later on, removing the scaffold of the card and just having children form their names with the individual let- ters and then write their name in their journals.

Label the Room. A popular activity is to take five to ten cards on which labels of objects in the room can be written. Take the children on a walkabout, asking them what they would like to label. Stop at each place, print the name of the object, saying the letter. Hold it up. Have the children say the name of the object and the name of the letters (e.g., "chair, c - h - a - i - r, chair!"). Help the children tape the card to the object. Later, walk and read the room. When children have grown completely familiar with the labels, remove them to a place in the room for familiar words and relabel the room.

Upper- and Lowercase Demo.   Choose a letter that begins one of the children's name (e.g., J). Say, "When I write Jamiel's name, I have to start it with an uppercase J. Watch [make uppercase letter]. When I start a sentence, I use uppercase, too. Watch while I write the sentence *Jack jumped high.* But look, if it doesn't start a sentence or it isn't someone's name, I can use the lowercase. See it right here [point out the word *jumped*]. I'm going to write the uppercase J here and the lowercase j right beside it [Jj]. Before you go to snack today, come up and write either the uppercase J or the lowercase j. Which will you write? Charron, you may start."

Opinion Surveys.   Have each child think of a question (e.g., Do you have a dog? Do you still take a nap? Do you like to eat vegetables?). Have them dictate it to you or write it if they can. Have them draw a line down the center of their paper and write "YES" on one side and "NO" on the other. Have them survey one another, with children writing their names under the appropriate column, depending on their opinion about the question. This can be made into a class book.

Name in Paint.   Provide pots of colored paint and cotton swabs. Have children dip the cotton swabs into the paint and paint their names. They can also have other children write their names on the paper in different colors as a souvenir to take home and read to their families. They can also paint their names as large as possible on a sheet of paper on the easel.

Sidewalk Chalk. Supply children with chalk and have them make an illustration on the sidewalk, sign their name, and write anything they can about what they drew. Invite parents to come watch the event.

Self-portraits/Family Portraits. Have children draw pictures of themselves, label them with their name, and either dictate information about themselves to the teacher or write something about themselves. Have them draw a family portrait and label the people in the picture.

Celebrated Letter. Draw a letter, both uppercase and lowercase (use the terminology) on the easel. Talk about the name of the letter (children need to learn the name of each letter as well as the sound it makes) and the sound it makes. Ask children to generate as many words as they can think of that start with that sound. For very young children, the teacher can draw a rebus figure to go along with the word to remind the children of what the word says. Keep the sheet out in the classroom so that children can reread it during the week.

Write for Real Purposes. Linda Brooke, an absolutely great kindergarten teacher at Cornerstone School in Ocala, Florida, has her children writing for real purposes. She has them writing notes home to their families, spelling as well as they can: "DON'T SEND REPORTS OF MY BEHAVEVING." "Mommy I wnt to red the majk flt ples Love Julia." They write about baby bunnies for sale ("Baby Bunys for sele for free. Sine-up"), and who should be next in line at an activity ("I am nexst Kristina"; Figures 3.6, 3.7, 3.8, and 3.9).

FIGURE **3.6**

Writing for real
purposes: "Don't
send reports of my
behaving."

FIGURE **3.7**

"Mommy, I want to
read the *Magic
Flute*, please. Love,
Julia."

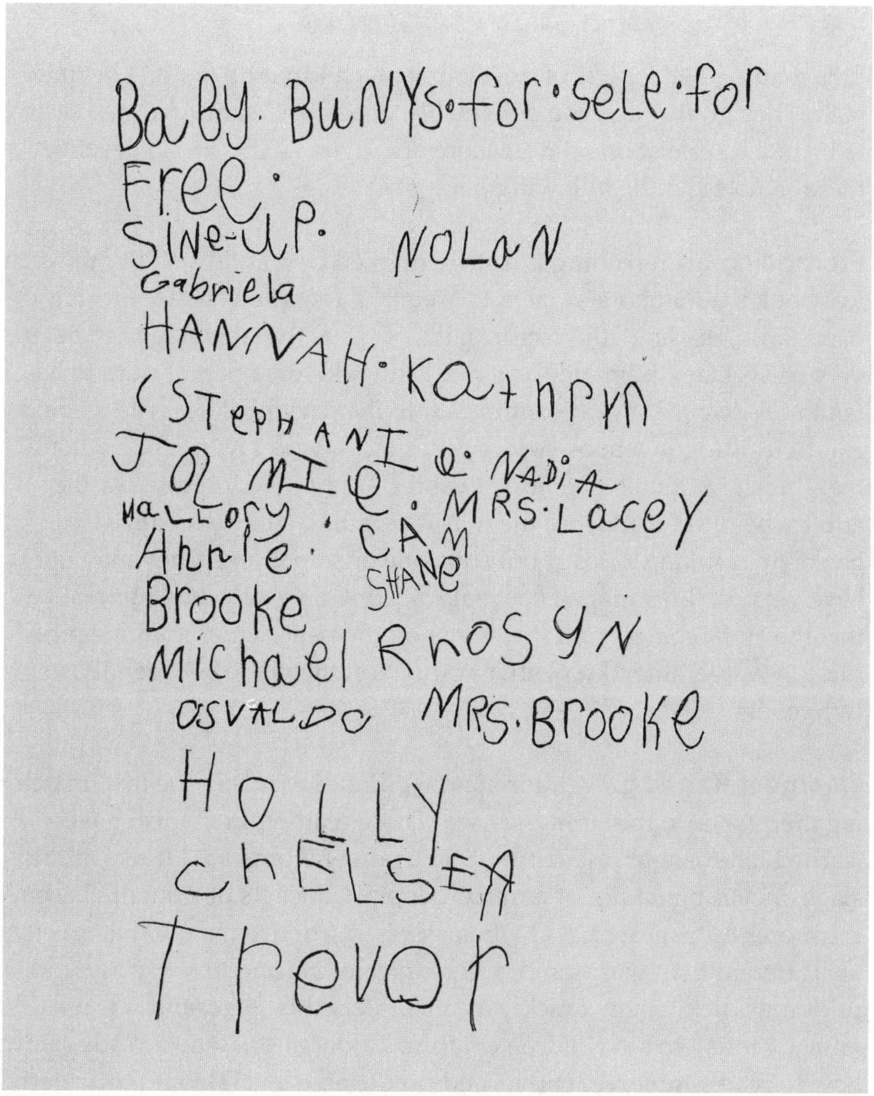

BaBy. BuNys.for.sele.for
Free.
SiNe-up. NoLaN
Gabriela
HANNAH. KatnrYn
(STEPHANIe NADiA
Jo MIe. MRS.Lacey
HaLLory. CAm
AhnIe. SHANe
Brooke
Michael RnosYN
OSVALDO MRS.Brooke
HOLLY
CHELSEA
TrevOr

FIGURE **3.8**

Children develop a
sign-up list to take
home a baby
bunny.

I am
nexst
KristINA

FIGURE **3.9**

"I am next. Kristina"

Early Reading Development

Like many other aspects of development, children do not just begin to read. They go through some definable stages, and some children seem to be in a couple at one time. Moore and Lyon (2005, 73–74) describe these as noted in the following paragraphs.

Prereading.   Prereading is a stage marked by a child's ability to listen to a book read aloud and even to "retell" a favorite book by turning pages and "reading" the pictures. It's obvious that this stage can begin very early, even in infancy as a child snuggles on a parent's lap to listen to *Goodnight Moon.* It continues into the preschool years as we find children sitting in a book corner "reading" a very favorite book aloud that they have almost memorized and sounding very much like the adult who often reads it to them. At this point, children realize that books do contain stories about someone or something. They may not have very well-developed concepts of print, and they may not realize that the story comes from the words on the page rather than the pictures; however, they know that a story is somewhere between those two covers.

Emergent Reading.   Children now point to words in the text, matching their voice to the print they see. Those reading in English have learned left-to-right orientation. Some power words are known at this stage, including names of familiar people. Concepts of print are becoming more sophisticated, and when assessed, children know that letters are different than words and different from one another. Exposure to print may dictate how quickly a child enters this stage, and it is not unusual today to see children entering kindergarten who already know how to read simple, repetitive, and predictable text. This is particularly true if they have attended literacy-rich preschools.

Early Reading.   Reading is becoming more strategic by this stage, and these children are no longer bound by reliance on sight words. Instead, they figure out words they haven't read before in three primary ways (Ehri & Roberts, 2006, 115):

1. *Decoding.* Decoding words involves sounding out letters and blending them to form recognizable spoken words. This may be accom-

plished either by transforming **graphemes** into a blend of phonemes or by pronouncing and blending larger spelling patterns.

2. *Analogy.* Reading words by analogy involves applying parts of known words to read new words—for example, reading faint by analogy to paint.

3. *Prediction.* Predicting words involves combining cues from the surrounding context and partial letter cues in spellings to anticipate the identity of words.

You'll see some early decoding in kindergarteners, because they know the sounds of many letters and can stretch out words and use context and pictures to figure out others. Being able to see smaller words within the larger word is also helpful, and they are becoming acquainted with word parts, such as prefixes and suffixes. Some discover onset and rime or word families (*will, bill, fill, kill*), leading to beginning analogy skill. Although predicting a word by using the first letter is more often wrong than right at first, children soon learn to combine that strategy with others to improve their accuracy rates. Most of these readers are in the first grade, but again, you may find that some of your kindergarten children are developing these abilities, particularly by the end of the year.

Transitional Reading.   Learned decoding strategies, familiarity with the reading process in general and in practice, and greater development of vocabulary all come together at this stage to produce a more complex and able reader. Fluidity, rate, efficiency, and comprehension are characteristic of these children who are usually found at the end of first grade and throughout grade two. It is the child who is in grade two who is still struggling with these skills that we need to pay very close attention to in terms of both informal and formal assessment.

Carol Seefeldt (2005) has advocated bringing back the language experience approach (LEA), a shared activity between teacher and beginning readers. It involves using common experiences the children have together (such as visiting the firehouse, going to the pumpkin farm) and using that topic to write about what they learned. It really is the know–want–learn (KWL) approach being used with children before, during, and after a project to document what they already knew (or thought they knew), what they want to find out, and finally what they learned. The stories, lists, and other suggestions from the children are written down and reread by the teacher and children. Because the vocabulary came from them, and the writing reflects their own ideas, they find it fairly easy to read back. Children with minimal skills find safety in the "group read." Children with more sophisticated or advanced skills step out to read a part of the chart or story and are paid great attention by the other children who are eager to learn "to do it, too."

Reading for meaning should always be in the child's mind, and this gets easier as word attack skills sharpen. Along the way, however, comprehension of what has just been read by the child or to the child can be addressed. Teachers can create simple story webs with children following the reading of a familiar book. Certain children can be given individual laminated cards prior to the story, on which there is printed (with rebus pictures) the words FAVORITE CHARACTER or SETTING or PROBLEM or SOLUTION, as well as other aspects of the story. After the story has been read, the child holding the card is called on for a response. Lots of discussion can follow any story, and it should be a relaxed conversation, much as would occur at the dinner table with adults. It should be allowed to wander a bit, with children contributing bits and pieces of their own experiences that were stimulated by the book.

The following are a number of ideas about working with preschoolers and kindergarteners to move them from one stage of reading to another:

1. Develop an environment that is rich in print. Immerse children in print that is both functional and/or illustrative: labels, lists, charts, books, children's written or dictated work and drawings, songs, nursery rhymes, finger plays, interactive charts, poems, job charts, daily schedules, signs, tape recorders and headphones, computers and software, big books, games, class rules (that children have helped to generate), reference materials, menus, and logographic print in the housekeeping area (cereal boxes, fast food boxes, telephone books, recipe books, newspapers, magazines). Have name cards at the snack table. Have children wear name tags every day (showing in front so other children can read them), selecting their own each morning as soon as they come in. Label the room and refer to the labels. For example, if you have a theme of Goldilocks and the three bears, turn the

housekeeping area into a bear's home and label chairs "Papa Bear's Chair," "Mama Bear's Chair," and "Baby Bear's Chair." Have organized shelves of no fewer than 90 narrative and information books and color-coded baskets of books that range from simple to more diffi-cult. Acquaint the children with what the colors mean. Display books attractively, setting them up with covers showing.

2. Read daily from big, oversize books with repetitive phrasing so that children can read interactively with you. Point to individual words only until children recognize that there is a space between every word and then move to running your hand underneath words to encourage more fluid reading. Make these books available to children in the reading center. They love to get together on the floor with a big book and look at it together.

3. Read daily from a variety of other books and genres. Before readings do a silent picture walk through some books to build chil-

dren's interest in listening to the story. Use wordless picture books so that chil-dren can make up a story from the pic-tures. Read predictable texts and encourage children to become involved in rhyme, rhythm, and repetition. Use information books frequently to build children's vocabulary and conceptual information in science, math, social stud-ies, and (social–emotional issues. Make up stories or tell familiar stories (e.g., *Jack and the Bean Stalk*) that you tell without the use of a book. Encourage

children to do the same. Use a lot of ABC books with the children to encourage identification of letters. As you read a page, encourage children to add a couple of words they know that begin with that same letter sound. Take time during center time to sit in a quiet corner and read to a couple of children who would like to hear a special book. Read as often during the day as you can, but always at least once in the morning and once again in the afternoon.

4. Teach concepts of print via the big books, making it easier for children to see where to begin reading, where to go next, the front and back of the book, the title, punctuation, one letter, two letters, and so forth. Teach them that books in English go from front to back, that print is organized from left to right and from top to bottom, that words are the things we read (not the pictures), that letters stand for the sounds we say, and that there is a space between each of the words.

5. Point to words only until children understand; then move to underscoring words by moving your hand underneath them so that children don't learn to read words, but phrases and sentences instead.

6. Teach children about story elements, such as characters, vocabulary, setting, events in a story, problems, and solutions.

7. We know that fluency in reading requires accuracy, speed and expression—and these are our goals with children. However, at the preschool level, we need to slow down to allow children to coordinate eye movements left to right and to match speech with print in a one-to-one manner (Moore & Lyon, 2005, 68). However, when a child is able to do this, it will be important not to point at single words so as not to encourage single reading of words, rather than phrases. At this point, run your hand smoothly (but slowly) underneath the line of print and encourage children to do the same.

8. Children can discover on their own a lot about literacy, but some literacy content requires targeted exposure and needs to be taught directly or children will not discover the knowledge. Included are letter names, the concept

that spoken words are made up of a series of individual sounds, the alphabetic principle, phonemic awareness, the relationship between oral language and print, and letter–sound association. These must be taught, keeping in mind DAPs, for the child will need experience with these to profit from later reading instruction (Schickedanz, 2003).

Suggested Activities to Enhance Early Reading Skills, Including Sight Word Recognition, Beginning Decoding Skills, Story Element Recognition, and Comprehension

Alphabet Boxes.   Place 26 small boxes together in a row. Label them with the letters of the alphabet. Have children collect small objects from the room that begin with the letter and place them in the appropriate box. When reading the room, stop at the alphabet boxes and select several, looking at what has been collected. After children are writing, have them take one of the boxes and see if they can write a word for each object in the box.

Outdoor Letter and Name Search.   Place different letters in places on the playground and have children go on a letter hunt, much as you would organize an Easter egg hunt. Have them take a small basket to collect their letters. Gather them together to show one another which letters they were able to find. Make sure that all children are successful in finding at least a few. You can vary this in any number of ways: Have children search for their own names or other children's names, words that are found on the word wall, only one letter (such as lots of the letter S hidden in many places) if they are very young, or only curvy letters or only straight letters. There are lots of ways to play the game.

Name Recognition.   When dismissing children from a large group (or at the end of the day or at lunchtime), hold up a card with a child's name printed on it. To expand after they begin to recognize others' names, tell them, "This morning, I'll hold up a name, but I'll call on someone else to tell me what the friend's name is."

Name Memory Game. Use sets of children's pictures with names printed underneath as a memory game, including only four or fewer sets to begin with and then expanding as children's memory skills and reading ability increase. After a while, use only names, eliminating pictures.

Puppet Drama. Provide stick puppets for children that are based on a familiar story (e.g., *Goldilocks and the Three Bears*). Have the children retell the story, using the puppets' "voices." One child can be selected to

be the narrator to retell the story, while the other children act out what the narrator says. Children can also pretend they are the person or animal and respond to questions the teacher asks them about their involvement in the story (children love to use "fake voices" for this). For example, the teacher could ask, "Goldilocks, how did you feel when you woke up and saw Baby Bear looking at you?" "Papa Bear, how did you come to build your house in the middle of the woods?" "Baby Bear, what did you think when you saw your broken chair?"

Word Sort. Provide a set of cards on which are printed short words, each of which begins with one of three different letters (e.g., cat, dog, mom, dad, can, my, car, mud, me). Have children sort the words into three different piles. Have them write the sets of words in their journals, underlining the first letter that is the same as all other words in that list.

Letter Detective. Purchase a set of "detective glasses" (sunglasses at the Dollar Store) that can be used by a small group of children to go on a letter-detecting mission. On paint stirrers, print an uppercase letter on one side and the same letter in lowercase on the other side. Have the children select one of these "letter-identifying sticks" from a pail holding them and tell them to begin their mission to find the particular letter somewhere in the room, alerting you when they have discovered one. You should get involved, actively watching the detectives and responding enthusiastically to children's "finds." To extend this, children can partner up, with one child holding the paint stick and another child recording on a clipboard the word that they found.

Literacy Detective.   Using a large chart on which a familiar song, finger play, or poem is written, ask, "Who can find . . ."

the first word on the page we are going to read

where I go next

the last word on this page

a letter they know

a word they know

the letter with which their first name begins

a letter in their name

the letter with which their last name begins

their favorite letter

the letter with which their friend's name begins

the letter _____ (you name the letter)

the letter with the sound _____ (you name the sound)

a letter after the letter _____

a lowercase letter

an uppercase or capital letter

a small word

a long word

a color word

a word that begins with _____

a word with _____ somewhere in the middle

a word that ends with _____

a word that means about the same as _____

a word that rhymes with _____

a word that is the opposite of _____

an action word

the name of a person, place, or thing

a word with the ending (-ing, -ly, -ed)

a period, question mark, quotation marks, exclamation mark, or contraction

Do only five to eight of these per day, depending on the children's interest. There is high interest in this activity.

Interactive Charts.   Using a familiar rhyme or finger play, develop a chart for which one of the words can be changed in a number of ways. For example, old MacDonald had a farm, and on this farm he had a _____. Make a pocket to hold the selected word and another to hold cards with a number of different words (in this case, dog, cat, cow, pig, rooster, chicken, hen, and so on). The child selects a word, places it in the pocket, and reads the entire phrase. Then substitute another word, reading the entire phrase with the new word. Children enjoy working in pairs for this activity, alternating reading.

Nursery Rhyme Shadow.   Make up two sets of exact strips for each line in a familiar nursery rhyme. Color code these for the youngest children (e.g., first line in red, second line in blue, third in yellow). Place one set in a pocket chart, with an empty row underneath each strip. In small group, read the rhyme a few times. Give each child a strip to match with those in the pocket chart. After they have done this a few times, cut the second set of strips into smaller phrases or words to make the matching more difficult. After a while, make all the strips the same color, so that they can no longer depend on color as a clue.

Animal Facts.   Erica Poindexter, a teacher in Michigan State University's Child Development Laboratory, has cardboard animals that she's created that are about four feet high. They hold fact sheets about themselves in front of their bodies or clutched in their mouth or in a paw. For example, a stately Emperor penguin holds a chart that says, "Hi. My name is Emperor penguin. I eat fish and squid. I live in the Antarctic. I love cold water!" When she introduces the children to these characters, she places the animals around the room and takes the children on a room walk, stopping at each animal to read their message about themselves. This is a great way to integrate life sciences and literacy in young children. This idea can be varied to introduce other factual material in an interesting way.

Climb the Mountain.   Draw a mountain or hill on an easel sheet. String letters randomly from the bottom of the hill, up and over the top, and down to the bottom again. See if the child can climb the mountain by naming the letters (or naming the sound each makes). On a subsequent mountain, place the names of their classmates to see if they can identify them. Later, substitute some of the anchor words that make up 25 percent of all spoken language (and, I, a, is, you, of, that, in, to, the, it, am, look, this, here, up, come, see, we, at, on, like, me, my, go) to see if they can climb through them.

Disappearing Letters.   On a sunshiny day, supply children with pails of water and large paintbrushes. Have them make letters on the sidewalk or playground and watch the letters disappear in the sun.

Story Listening Center.   Supply taped stories, copies of the books, and headphones for one or two children to listen to the story. There should be a signal when children are supposed to turn the page. These can be purchased commercially, but teachers can also tape familiar stories.

Story Webbing/Graphic Organizers/ Story Murals.   Use any webbing method or graphic organizer to set out various story elements (characters, setting, title, illustrator, problem, solution, events, and so on). Have children create a mural, illustrating a story in a sequence. The teacher can divide a long mural into a number of sections and label each, beginning with the title and then the subsequent events, one in each section. The children can illustrate the sections. This can be hung at the children's eye level so that they can retell the story.

Doll House Match.   Create the outline of a doll house with four rooms on a large piece of tagboard. Label the upper two rooms

"Bedroom 1" and "Bathroom." Label the two lower rooms "Living Room" and "Kitchen." Place about five Velcro buttons in the center of each room, lined up. Create corresponding strips with names of fixtures or furniture (which also have pictures of the item) that would go in each room and put Velcro buttons on the back of each one. Line these up on the side of the tagboard, outside the house. Invite the children to place the fixtures or furniture in the right room. Later, encourage the children to say the name of the item and spell it before placing it in the right room. For a writing activity, have children draw an outline of the house in their journal, position the strips, and write the names in the rooms.

Object/Person Label.   Using the same idea presented earlier, create a large character from a book familiar to the children (e.g., Goldilocks, Papa Bear, Wild Thing). Place Velcro dots in appropriate places on the character. Develop word strips such as "eye," "nose," "ear," "arm," "leg," and so on, with Velcro dots on the back so that the children can attach them to the character or figure.

Story Sequencing.   Work with an individual child or small group of children. Tell them, "I'm going to tell you a story and then I'll give you four pictures from the story I told you. I want you to line them up in the right order. Try to remember what happens first in the story, next in the story, almost at the end of the story, and then at the end. Ready? Listen to my story."

Flannel Board Stories.   Wrap a three-foot-by-three-foot section of plywood with flannel. Make up large manila envelopes that have a picture of a familiar book glued on the front. Inside, place a paperback copy of the book and a number of flannel figures that the children can use to retell the story. Demonstrate the activity in a large group, emphasizing to the children the necessity of placing the flannel figures back in the envelope when they are done and clipping it to the board so that other children can use it. Place the flannel board on the floor in a quiet place and clip the envelope to the flannel board with a clothespin. Have enough room so that one or two children can sit and recreate the story.

Start at the Star.   To teach the concept of print about where to start reading on a page, place a gummed star at the beginning of the story on each page of a big book. Remind the children, "I'm going to start reading here, right where the star is on this page."

There are any number of literacy activity books and commercial materials that you can purchase to help you with ideas, but most of the best ones will come from your own creative thinking. What's important is to remember the reason you're structuring the activity in the first place—namely, to build strong literacy skills and concepts in the children. Cutesy activities and materials that lack real purpose in terms of advancing language and literacy in the children should be avoided and should never replace deeper, broader activities.

Chapter 4

The Child's World outside the Classroom

Involving Families as Partners in the Literacy Process

From their earliest years, children's emergent literacy and later school success is greatly affected by their environment. Parents who read and talk with their children daily, ask questions, listen, and tell stories are creating an environment that builds and supports their children's early learning and interest in reading. Children who grow up in less stimulating or unsafe environments are often ill prepared to enter preschool and kindergarten with the foundational skills acquired by their peers. Teachers see these differences among children every day in their classrooms and work hard to help children learn new skills and behaviors; however, they also know that the school setting alone is not enough. The link between the quality of children's home experiences and school readiness has focused attention on the benefits of creating stronger home–school connections to build and reinforce children's learning. Numerous studies have shown that such involvement has immediate and long-lasting benefits for children, including

- Higher grades and test scores

- Better attendance and more homework completed

- Fewer placements in special education

- More positive attitudes and behaviors

- Higher graduation rates and greater enrollment in postsecondary education (Davis, 2000)

However, forging strong and genuine school–family partnerships is tough business and adds considerably to your growing list of responsibilities. Building strong linkages with families requires commitment, time, and intentional planning. Faced with many other pressures and increasingly complex demands to improve instructional practice at both the preschool and kindergarten levels, how can you find the time to involve families in meaningful ways that will support children's growth? Given your limited time, are there some activities and practices more effective than others in gaining parental support? If you have not previously had much involvement with parents or caregivers, what are some easy ways to begin creating a partnership with families? In this chapter we give you some practical suggestions that teachers we know have successfully used to improve their working relationships with families.

However configured, however constrained, families come with their children to school. Even when they do not come in person, families come in children's minds and hearts and in their hopes and dreams. They come with the children's problems and promise. Without exception, teachers and administrators have explicit or implicit contact with their students' families every day.

JOYCE EPSTEIN

Welcoming Families to the Preschool and Kindergarten Environments

Successful parental involvement often depends on how welcome we make parents feel right from the start—when they take part in early opportunities to visit the program or classroom, or speak to teachers and administrators (U.S. Department of Education, 1997). Typically, these early opportunities begin with preschool or kindergarten fairs and orientation sessions held prior to a new school year. During these sessions, parents may learn more about the school program, including daily schedules, curriculum, transportation, and school resources; receive suggestions

On June 1st Ms. Poindexter joined Jon, Saad, Sam, Trevor and Paola in the block area while they built with train tracks. She prompted the children by saying "we only have one traffic sign for the trains, how can we get the trains to stop and go?" The children suggested creating their own signs to use. The materials were provided which included, various colors and shapes of paper, popsicle sticks, markers and tape. The children worked together to create their own stop/go signs to use with the trains. Saad also wrote out signs to label the buildings the train passed by.

on how to help their child at home; and find out about volunteer opportunities in the program or how to become involved in parent–teacher organizations or parent councils. Some programs and schools may also offer expanded orientations that include informal or more formal assessments of children, while parents learn more about community programs or services and ways they can help prepare their child for school. Representatives from local community agencies and school district support personnel are often invited to participate in these events. This summer, Haslett's Early Childhood Center turned the usual ice cream social into a literacy ice cream social. Families and community partners were invited to a schoolwide, indoor and outdoor activity hour during which children's growth in literacy was on display—in the classroom, the hallways, and on the playground.

When these early experiences at the program or school level are positive, families feel welcome in the school and are much more likely to continue their participation and interaction during the coming year. They experience less anxiety about their child's transition to school, secure in the knowledge that they will have an important voice in what happens to their children.

Constructing early welcoming experiences requires that we understand the increasingly diverse economic and social backgrounds of the families and children in our programs and classrooms. Based on research and self-report data of parenting practices related to early literacy, we know there are substantial differences related to the income and educational levels of parents (Hart & Risley, 2003; U.S. Department of Education, National Center for Statistics, 2006). Learning about the backgrounds of your children's parents can help you build a parent involvement program that will be meaningful to your children's parents—emphasizing what they can do to support their children's learning now.

In working with families and children from different cultures, Volk and Long (2005, 12–19) caution against making assumptions in parenting beliefs and practices about children from different cultural backgrounds. They have identified a number of myths about bilingual families in their research on language and literacy of young bilingual children that can interfere with establishing effective parent–school partnerships:

Myth 1: *Families from marginalized communities do not value education.* What they found: All the participants in their studies valued education highly and believed that education was important for doing well in life and work. Most parents noted that being schooled is only part of being *bien educado* (well educated)—that is, an educated person also knows how to act respectfully with others.

Myth 2: *If parents cared about their children, they would read to them every day and teach them basic skills at home, using the methods teachers use. Parents from marginalized communities do not know how to teach like teachers.* What they found: Parents supported their children as literacy learners in multiple, effective ways. Sometimes their methods were similar to those used by teachers, and sometimes they were different. Nonetheless, many engaged their children in family activities that involved literacy, such as reading letters and the Bible.

Myth 3: *Children from marginalized communities participate in few, if any, literacy interactions and activities at home.* What they found: The children participated in many interactions and activities at home (Figure 4.1).

Myth 4: *Children from marginalized communities have few literacy resources.* What they found: Children had abundant human and literacy resources. They were surrounded by networks of support, people of varying ages and abilities who helped the children develop literacy. The children and their siblings and friends often engaged in sociodramatic play, using literacy practices drawn from their cultural worlds. Playing school was a favorite, but the children also played McDonald's and church, with plenty of reading, singing, preaching, and reciting memorized prayers.

Myth 5: *Children from marginalized communities do not use effective strategies to support their own literacy learning, much less the learning of others.* What they found: The children made skillful use of strategies learned at school, at home, and in the community to support their own learning and that of others. In both kindergartens peers were observed helping each other during formal and informal literacy activities. Whether monolingual or bilingual, the children moved in and out of the teacher and learner roles, providing peer assistance as follows:

- Engaging in side-by-side reading, picture reading, writing, and drawing
- Translating and clarifying
- Providing demonstrations of appropriate literacy behaviors

- Doing homework

- Reviewing schoolwork, reading teacher letters

- Practicing school-related skills

- Talking about schoolwork, and reading and writing

- Using workbooks

- Looking at and reading books (their own and others' picture books and school books, library books, coloring books, address books, and dictionaries)

- Listening to books and letters read aloud by others

- Reading/writing greeting cards

- Enacting literacy-related cultural roles: playing "school," "church," and "McDonald's"

- Watching TV and videos, for entertainment and language learning

- Playing with a mini computer, video games, a musical keyboard with letters

- Playing children's card games and board games, doing puzzles, collecting baseball cards

- Reading/listening to Bible passages and Bible commentaries

- Memorizing psalms to recite in church

- Writing, reciting, singing, and listening to poems, stories, and songs from families' cultures, from school, and from popular culture, some created by the children

- Drawing and writing with crayons, markers, pencils, and pens in notebooks and on pads and loose paper

FIGURE **4.1**

Children's Home Literacy Interactions and Activities (Volk & Long, 2005)

- Enacting literacy-related cultural roles by playing "school" and "home," and during dramatic play, drawing on popular culture and on books read in school

- Offering to help

- Demonstrating classroom routines
- Viewing English language learners as possessing expertise

The National PTA (2004) has developed a checklist that programs and schools can use to assess the degree to which their programs evidence family-friendly practices. Their checklist reminds us that we need to evidence our beliefs that parents are valued and welcome partners in the program in the following ways:

- Regular, two-way, and meaningful communication is practiced.
- Responsible parenting is promoted and supported.
- Parents play an integral role in assisting student learning.
- Parents are welcome in the school, and their support and assistance are sought.
- Parents are full partners in the decisions that affect children and families.
- Community resources are made available to strengthen school programs, family practices, and student learning.

A Framework for Parent Involvement

Epstein (2002) has developed a framework for six types of involvement for home–school partnerships, with examples of what you can do within each category to promote involvement (see Figure 4.2). Realistically, the challenges in trying to implement these types of family involvement are many. Providing information may be difficult when some families do not speak English or read well. Initially, at least, there may be latent hostility to the school environment if family members did not have a successful academic experience themselves. Families may disagree about turf issues or have culturally different views of how children should be disciplined. Life in some families may be so chaotic that just getting a child to school on time constitutes involvement and support. Despite these difficulties, it is worth the time and effort it takes to obtain true parental involvement in terms of building solid comprehensive and in-depth literacy support for children. Well-designed and organized partnerships send a message to families: We care what happens to your children; thus, we care about you.

1. *Parenting*—Helping all families establish home environments to support children as students; suggesting home conditions that support learning at each grade level; holding workshops and lending videos on parenting and child rearing; providing family literacy education; suggesting family support programs to assist with health, nutrition, and other services; conducting home visits to help with transitions

2. *Communicating*—Designing effective forms of school-to-home and home-to-school communications about school programs and their child's progress; holding conferences, with follow-up as needed; assisting families with language translators as needed; sending home weekly or monthly folders of student work for review and comments; promoting **student-led conferencing** and pickup of report cards; scheduling regularly useful notices, memos, phone calls, and newsletters; providing clear information on programs, activities, and school policies

3. *Volunteering*—Recruiting and organizing parent help and support for teachers, administrators, students, and other parents; providing a parent room or family center for volunteer work meetings and resources for families; conducting annual postcard surveys identifying all available talents, times, and locations of volunteers; establishing class parents, a telephone tree, or other structures to provide all families with needed information; devising parent patrols or other activities to aid safety and operation of school programs

4. *Learning at home*—Providing information and ideas about how to help children with homework and other curriculum-related activities, decisions, and planning information on skills required for children in all subjects at each grade, homework policies, and how to monitor and discuss school work at home; providing information on how to help children improve skills; scheduling regular homework that requires children to discuss and interact with families on what they are learning; preparing calendars with activities for parents and children to do at home or in the community; hosting family math, science, and reading activities at school; preparing summer learning

FIGURE **4.2**

Epstein's Six Types of Parent Involvement with Examples of Teacher Practice to Support Involvement

(continues)

packets or activities; encouraging family participation in setting learning goals for children

5. *Decision making*—Including parents in school decisions;
developing parent leaders and representatives; being active
in PTA/PTO, parent advisory council, or committees (e.g., curriculum, safety, personnel); joining independent advocacy
groups and working for school reform and improvement;
attending district-level councils and committees; disseminat-
ing information on school or local elections for school representatives; building networks to link all families with parent
representatives

6. *Collaborating with the
   community*—Identifying
   and integrating
   resources and services
   from the community to
   strengthen school pro-
   grams, family practices,
   and children's learning
   and development; pro-
   viding information for
   children and families on
   community health, cul-
   tural, recreational,
   social support, and
   other programs or ser-
   vices that link to learning skills and talents;
   fostering service inte-

gration through partnerships (school, civic, counseling, cultural, health, recreation); providing service to the community
by children, families, and schools (e.g., recycling, art, music,
drama); encouraging alumni participation in school programs
for children

FIGURE **4.2**

(Continued)

Planning Your Parent Involvement Program

A successful parent involvement program welcomes parents from the beginning continues to build a strong relationship with parents throughout the school year, and focuses on children's learning. As you develop your plan to enhance parental involvement in your classroom, reflect on the degree to which your current orientation program builds a welcoming climate for parents to the school and your classroom. Do many parents and children participate in the orientation? Do you get information from the parents that will help you in planning culturally sensitive activities for the new school year? Does the program help your parents and children learn more about what to expect in the coming year? What changes can be made to make this activity more useful?

When planning your parent involvement program, choose activities that you will enjoy and that will make the best use of your time. Think about successful programs conducted by you or colleagues in the past. Were they well received by parents? Did they accomplish what you wanted? If not, why not? Are there ways to build on successful elements of previous programs? Additionally, keep the following general considerations in mind as you plan your program for the year:

1. Choose activities that will focus on specific knowledge and skills your children need in your classroom. Parents and children will enjoy and learn more from activities that actively engage both parent and child.

2. Find ways to reduce or eliminate barriers to parent involvement (such as lack of time for both you and parents, and transportation).

3. Try to combine your programs with other school activities or functions to save time for parents and yourself.

4. Share the workload of planning and conducting activities by recruiting other teachers or program specialists in the same grade level or interest area to work with you.

5. Organize your time by developing a calendar of intentional activities throughout the year.

6. Select activities in which parents have already indicated an interest through an interest survey.

7. Provide translators in more than one language, if needed, for bilingual support and materials.

A communication plan is also an important part of your parent program. It is not always easy to communicate with parents, particularly when there are language differences or low literacy levels. Many families in our program did not have phones or they changed telephone numbers several times during the course of the year. Your plan should take into consideration the backgrounds of your student population and their families to determine the best methods of reaching out to them. In all communications you will want to reflect a caring and welcoming tone. Mendoza, Katz, Robertson, and Rothenberg (2003, 4) offer the following suggestions for building good parent communications:

■ Convey mutual trust and respect.

■ Maintain regular, two-way, meaningful communication between home and school.

■ Focus on communication that is for "the good of the child."

■ Use a variety of connecting methods such as notices, phone calls, conferences, memos, conversations, and other venues.

■ Recognize and work to overcome potential barriers to communication, such as language differences and/or low literacy.

■ Become familiar with the information needs and the patterns of information seeking and issues in the community served.

Suggestions for Enhancing Preschool and Kindergarten Orientation

If not already included in your school's orientation program, use this time to introduce parents to your classroom goals and objectives for the year. Provide them with a take-home packet of information containing suggestions for things they can do at home to support their child's learning. Include in that packet a list of suggested books, educational CDs, and television programs to read or view over the summer for parents to read to their children, fun learning activities to do at home with their children, and a calendar of community enrichment events that they can share with their child. Libraries are a wonderful resource for gathering this type of information. Free information is also available from the federal government or on many parent resource websites.

Use the orientation time to talk with parents to learn more about their backgrounds. Encourage them to talk about their child's previous learning experiences and exposure to books and language (for suggestions on questions to ask, see home visiting section later in this chapter). Find out whether the child has any special needs or whether the parents have any concerns about their child's adjustment to school. This is a good time also to check on any special needs children may have or concerns of parents so that you can begin creating a plan for any special supports needed to assist the family even before the child comes to your classroom.

Include a survey for the parents to complete regarding the types of activities in which they would like to participate during the school year (Figure 4.3). Ask if parents are interested in educational workshops at

Main Street Preschool/Kindergarten Parent Resource Inventory

Dear Parents,

Our children enjoy seeing their parents and family members in our classroom. We invite you to share your interests and talents with us this year. Please indicate whether you would be interested and are able to share your time. The following are some possible areas, but please feel free to add other areas not included in this list. Thank you for helping us!

☐ I play an instrument _____

☐ I like to sing

☐ I like to cook or bake

☐ I can do folk dances

☐ I am a collector _____

☐ Other: _____

Parent's Name _____ Child's Name _____

Contact Information and Availability _____

FIGURE **4.3**

Parent Resource Inventory

school, work coming home from school, or parent–child activities in school. Do they prefer information or materials to be sent home? Some teachers have found it helpful to create a bank of special skills or talents that parents may contribute in the classroom. They use this information to invite parents in for special events. If you have children from different cultural backgrounds, sharing ethnic foods, customs, or clothing is a good way to help children learn about differences. Children enjoy seeing their family members in school and being a part of their school life.

Reaching out to parents and families in these ways will help families feel welcome in your classroom. They will sense your interest and willingness to have a partnership with them even before their child is in your classroom. What better way can there be to start out the new year!

Ideas for Parent Involvement Activities throughout the School Year

After the orientation, or if parents were unable to attend it, there are many more opportunities to increase your parent–home communication and involvement. One way is to look at your classroom as a home for your parents as well as their children. Help parents feel welcome by creating a special place for them designated as a "parent corner." You might only have room for a bulletin board, but the important thing is that parents know that this space is reserved for them. Try to set up the space near the front door of the classroom, where it will be easily accessible to parents when they pick up their child from school. Post parent information, news, and updates in this space or provide handouts on tips for children's learning. If you have space, create a nook with a bookcase where parents can check out or donate educational books, CDs, or videos. A parent volunteer can help with keeping the nook orderly and suggesting resources that parents would like.

The following examples are based on actual activities we have seen preschool and kindergarten teachers do in their classrooms. Some teachers invest more time than others. We suggest that you look at the list and pick activities that interest you. See how they work and add more as you become more comfortable.

- Create a calendar of activities that parents can do with their children to coincide with themes and objectives you will be covering during the year. Note: Parents receive lots of paper from school. When you send home information from you, always use the same color paper so that parents know this message is coming from you.

- Prepare a monthly newsletter emphasizing literacy goals for that month and how parents can help at home.

- Encourage parents to read daily to their children at home and to limit TV viewing. Suggest to parents that they watch programs with their child and ask questions about what is going on, why it is happening, and what they think will happen next.

- Create activity packets to go home periodically with children. Design these activities to encourage parent–child interaction. Send instructions with the kit. Include paper for children or parents to make hand-made books about family activities, children's favorite toys, vacations, favorite foods, or one that is "all about me." Include supplies for making simple puppets.

- Circulate a classroom backpack stuffed with books and games that rotates going home to all children. In our example in Figure 4.3, you send home a backpack containing a stuffed purple dinosaur, an informational book on dinosaurs, and a narrative book called *Dinosaur Island*. Include a notebook and the letter that appears in Figure 4.4.

- You can follow up on the backpack theme by sponsoring family reading nights, with everyone selecting a book from the classroom or library, or invite a storyteller to read. When you do this, provide a guide with questions for parents to ask their child. In this way, you will be modeling good practices. Make it a fun and relaxing event by setting up treats or snacks.

- Encourage parents to visit the classroom to see how you teach. Offer certain times that would be best for you or when you will be doing an activity that might be especially interesting to parents or other family members.

- Conduct workshops for parents that will help them work with their child at home. Interactive workshops with parents and children are fun and give you a chance to model practices. Involve parents and

Anytown Classroom

Dear Parents,

Hello from our class. This dinosaur's name is Purplesaurus. He will need very good care from your family this weekend. He likes to listen to the books he's brought with him. One is informational, called *Dinosaurs*. Another is fictional, called *Dinosaur Island*.

Please let Purplesaurus listen when you read these books to your child. Afterward, you will see in this notebook a question for you to answer that was written by the last family that Purplesaurus visited. Please work with your child to find the answer and write it after the question. Then, think of a question for the next family and write it down in this notebook.

Have fun with Purplesaurus. He will want to be back at school on Monday because he never misses school unless he is sick. So far, he's been very healthy.

P.S. Please don't feed Purplesaurus.

Question: Which type of dinosaur swallowed stones to help grind up food in its stomach?

Answer: _____

Question: _____

Answer: _____

FIGURE 4.4

Purplesaurus Home
Classroom Backpack

children in creating games to enhance literacy, such as make-it-and-take-it memory cards with letters and simple words, letter and word Bingo, or matching rhyming words and pictures. These games are fun and simple to do. Provide materials for making labels to place around the house to expand children's vocabulary.

- Periodically contact parents to let them know how the child is doing—don't wait for problems to occur. As one parent put it, "It would be wonderful if teachers would just pick up the phone and call parents. Direct verbal communication would be phenomenal. It would only take five minutes and this would be a start to making things comfortable for both parents and teachers."

■ Sponsor workshops for parents based on interests identified in the parent survey. Popular topics include child-rearing issues; nutrition, health, or safety; information on community services to help children and families; parenting skills; and child or adolescent development. Recruit guest speakers to address topics with which you are not familiar.

■ Send home information designed to promote learning at home (see the parent resource list at the end of the chapter). Anticipate and be prepared to answer questions like these: When should my child learn to write her name and how long will it take her to get it right? When should my child recognize the alphabet?

■ Hold potluck dinners before parent–teacher conferences (more easily arranged when conferences are student led) or other schoolwide events. Invite families to join the class for breakfast or lunch. Use this time to read a story and listen to songs or poems.

■ Create an end-of-the-year learning packet with an emphasis on literacy. Work with the kindergarten and first grade teachers to design activity packets to maintain learning over the summer. Suggest that parents investigate community programs such as those offered by public libraries or community youth programs that will reinforce children's learning.

Although these activities may seem overwhelming at first, it is important to remember that you only need to begin with a few that are best for you and your families. You will quickly be able to gauge others that can be added to benefit everyone. As Epstein (2001, 600–602) notes, it is important to remember that

■ These partnerships are about children and their success in school. Children are the reasons these partners communicate and work together.

■ These partnerships are for all families—not just for those families who are formally educated, easy to reach, or able to come often to school. These partnerships are important at all grade levels, from preschool through high school.

■ These partnerships should focus on results to help children succeed in school. They must include activities planned over time that will help promote, improve, or maintain school goals and high standards for school success.

The whole business of making a home visit is a statement of how much you care and respect this child. You take that first step and you meet children on their territory . . . . It is scary to walk into so many homes you have absolutely no idea about, but it does make a statement; and if the child does not pick up on that caring, the parents do, and it is conveyed back to the child. Home visits are the best way I can think of to say to that child, "You are important."

LYNNE JOHNSTON AND JOY MERMIN

For very young children, the home visit is a vital first contact with families; however, surveys indicate that very few teachers visit with children and parents on their turf (NCES, 1998). Home visits were required of the preschool and kindergarten teachers participating in our summer kindergarten transition project, and time was built into the schedule for teachers to conduct these visits. At first, there was some hesitancy on the part of the teachers to conduct home visits. However, after they began to make them, teachers found that they were extremely helpful. The following is a summary of the major benefits noted by teachers about their first home visits and their direct comments:

1. The visits improved their understanding of the child's environment and how the child functioned within it.

   "It helped to see what the home life actually looks like. The children were very proud of their homes."

   "Seeing the child's home environment helped to understand the child better."

2. It helped them to develop a closer relationship with the parent.

   "If I go on a home visit, they will back me up and be more involved later."

   "Parents were very friendly since they were on their home turf."

3. They were able to learn more from the parent about issues that might affect the child's school performance.

    "One on one, I find out a lot more information than parents provide on printed forms—speech, language needs, difficult parent situations."

4. The visit helped them gain parental support for the learning objectives of the program—in this case, early literacy and social competence.

    "I used the parent visit to communicate what kindergarten is all about."

    "Parents asked about supplies needed for school and what they could do at home."

Preparing for Your Home Visit

Let parents know that your ability to work most effectively with their children would be incomplete without the knowledge they can supply. Use this time to get to know the child—likes and dislikes, early learning experiences, favorite people and things, and any factors that may affect transition to the formal learning environment. Who are the other supportive people in the child's life outside the family? This can give you a cue about the kinds of supports parents may or may not have.

This is also a time when you can exchange particular information with parents and answer any questions they have about the school experience. Because our focus here is literacy, we suggest that it be made a priority during the visit. Underscore this theme by

1. Bringing a classroom book to read to the child during the visit. Pick one from your classroom and tell the child that this is one of the many books that he or she sees when he or she comes to school.

2. Providing paper and crayons or markers so the child can make a picture of his or her family while you talk with the parent. Ask the child to write his or her name on the picture. You can tell the child to watch for the picture on the first day of school: "It will be hanging in a special place, along with pictures made by all the other children who will be coming with you to school."

3. Preparing information and materials to enhance the child's emerging literacy that will be left with the family, including ideas for interactive parent–child experiences, and watching television.

Scheduling Home Visits

Routinely, these visits are best made before school begins. Some programs require home visits before school begins. Others have modified their calendars to allow time at the start of the new school year for these contacts. For example, a kindergarten calendar for the first week or two might be half days with children, with the other half day devoted to parent contact. However, if time is not available then or if class sizes are large, the visits may be spread out over the first several months of the school year or by invitation from parents after they have received an initial letter or telephone call.

Scheduling visits can be difficult and time-consuming. Tentative meeting dates may be arranged during the spring registration process and reconfirmed by telephone calls, postcards, or reminder letters over the summer. However, if you work in an area with high mobility, it may be difficult to get accurate addresses and phone numbers before children are actually in school. In this case, notes can go home with children during the first week of classes (Figure 4.5).

Let the parent know what to expect during the home visit when arranging the visit. If parents are reluctant to have the teacher in their home, or if there is a safety issue, a neutral site comfortable to the parent is a good alternative. These sites could include a local coffee shop, neighborhood park, or other place suggested by the parent. Plan to visit for no more than half an hour and make sure to inform the parent of the purpose.

Conducting a Home Visit

A half-hour visit is not much time. Think about what you want to accomplish during this time. Plan time to talk with the child and parent separately if possible. Talk with the child directly about what it will be like at school: "We have a table full of sand that you'll like, lots of books, and some great blocks and trucks." While the child is drawing or looking at a book you may have brought from school, learn more about the child from the parent and use this time to share expectations about the coming school year.

It is helpful to have a set of questions to help structure the visit. Some programs that routinely conduct home visits will have a standard set of questions on a form that you can complete during the visit. If you are interested in adopting this practice program- or schoolwide, meet

Main Street School

Anytown, USA

Dear _____   Date _____

I would like to welcome you and your child, _____, to my kindergarten classroom. To help make this a successful year, I would like to get to know you and your child better by visiting with you and your child in your home on _____. The visit will last about 30 minutes.

During this time, I will be sharing information about our classroom with you and your child, answering your questions about our program, and discussing your expectations for your child's learning this year. By working together, we can make this a successful year for your child.

Please let me know if this time and date will work for you. If not, I can be reached at _____ to reschedule. I look forward to seeing you soon.

Sincerely,

FIGURE **4.5**

Request for a
Home Visit

with others to find out the most valuable information that you will want to know. Remember always to ask parents if you may take notes during your conversation to help you remember what was said. Teachers in our project found the following questions particularly helpful:

- What are your child's favorite things?
- What does your child like to do?
- What do you like to do as a family?
- Does your child have any favorite stories, books, or songs?
- What were your favorite books as a child?
- Have you shared this book with your child?
- What does your child do well?
- What do you want your child to gain this year?

- Would you like to get ideas on how to help your child's learning at home?

Other questions that may be helpful to you if not already asked on other forms include

- How would you describe your child?
- With whom does the child spend time regularly?
- What are your child's favorite foods?
- Did your child attend any preschool program?
- If so, what did your child like best about preschool?
- Is there any health issue or special need that may affect your child's learning?
- What is the best way to contact you? Phone, notes home, mail, e-mail?

When you get back to school, keep information from the home visit in a personal file and refer to it during the school year. Use this information as you plan for continued contact with parents during the school year and to inform your classroom program and activities.

Commonly Asked Questions about Home Visits

When we began requiring home visits in our program, teachers had many questions about them. The following are examples of some of the most common questions.

Q: I understand that home visits are a good idea, but how can I find the time to do them?

A: We estimate that it will take about an hour per child—30 minutes travel time going and coming, and 30 minutes with parents/child. Moreover, it will take time to set up appointments and send reminder notes. Talk with your program or school administrator about the benefits of home visits and suggest that time be built into the school year calendar to do them, perhaps as a pilot if there is some reluctance. If this is not possible, make time. As one of our teachers put it, "You just have to find the time to do it." Spread it out over several months, whether at lunchtime or directly after school.

Q: I would like to try home visiting, but how do I start?

A: Think about what you want to accomplish during the visit and go prepared with activities for the child and a plan for discussion with the parent. If you are hesitant to go alone, invite someone else from school to go with you. This could be the school nurse, another teacher who might know the family, or a teaching assistant. You will find parents and children eager to meet with you and will soon feel comfortable meeting with them yourself.

Q: How do I start the conversation?

A: Begin by introducing yourself and expressing how happy you are to meet: "Hello, Mr. Jones, I'm Karen James and I'm so happy to meet with you and to have your daughter Leia in our classroom this year. I am meeting with all the kindergarten parents to . . ."

Q: How do I handle language barriers?

A: When setting up the appointment, ask if bilingual help is needed. Talk with program or school administrators to determine whether these services are available within your program. Sometimes, older children in the family or even neighbors may act as translators. If not, you can also check with community agencies to determine whether you can get assistance from them.

Q: I would like to visit all my families, but some parents are hesitant. What should I do?

A: Most parents of preschool and kindergarten students are eager to meet their child's teacher, but a few may be reluctant to have someone in their home. Offer to meet at an alternative site, including your classroom. Explain that you are meeting with all the parents to talk about learning objectives for the year. Focus on what you can do together to help their child succeed.

Q: What about working parents?

A: It may not be possible for parents to meet with you because of scheduling conflicts. Try a phone conference. Emphasize the questions that will help you the most and encourage parents to ask you questions.

Parent Resources

The following resources provide excellent and practical ideas for parents to help support their child's learning. They are available at no charge from EDPubs—free resources—at 1-877-4ED PUBS (433-7827) and on the Web at www.ed.gov/parents/academic/help/tools-for-success/index.html.

Helping Your Child Become a Reader—Other than helping your children to grow up healthy and happy, the most important thing you can do for them is to help them develop their reading skills. This booklet offers pointers on how to build the language skills of young children, and includes a list of typical language accomplishments for different age groups, suggestions for books, and resources for children with reading problems or learning disabilities.

Helping Your Child Succeed in School—Every child has the power to succeed in school and in life, and every parent, family member, and caregiver can help. This booklet provides parents with information, tools, and activities they can use in the home to help their child develop the skills critical to academic success.

Reading Tips for Parents—This document addresses topics such as: How Can I Help My Child Be Ready to Read and Ready to Learn? How Do I Know a Good Early Reading Program When I See One? Other topics include Simple Strategies for Creating Strong Readers and The Five Essential Components of Reading.

A Child Becomes a Reader—Proven Ideas for Parents from Research— Kindergarten through Grade Three (available only online)—The road to becoming a reader begins the day a child is born and continues through the end of third grade. At that point, a child must read with ease and understanding to take advantage of the learning opportunities in fourth grade and beyond. This booklet offers advice for parents of children from grades K–3 on how to support reading development at home, and how to recognize effective instruction in their children's classrooms.

Put Reading First—Helping Your Child Learn to Read—This brochure, designed for parents of young children, describes the kinds of early literacy activities that should take place at school and at home to help children learn to read successfully. It is based on the findings of the National Reading Panel.

Chapter 5

Useful and Authentic Assessment Strategies

W hen good programs are set in place, good outcomes for children are predictable. To celebrate both good teaching and learning, we want to document that the children in our classrooms are increasing their skills in every area of emerging literacy. To do

Teachers must see the value of what they are doing and of the instruments they are using to assess their students.

JERRY ASLENGER

this, it's necessary to set up an organized and comprehensive assessment approach to keep track of each child's continuous progress. This should be a collaborative process, involving the children, their parents, and other professionals who play a supportive role in the child's life. We

agree with Winograd, Flores–Duenas, and Arrington (2003, 208–209), that best practices in assessment do the following:

- Focus on important goals and support meaningful student learning

- Are based on our most current and complete understanding of literacy and children's development

- Are based in the classroom, rather than imposed from outside

- Involve students in their own learning and enhance their understanding of their own development

- Use criteria and standards that are public, so that students, teachers, parents, and others know what is expected

- Start with what the students currently know

- Involve teachers (and often students) in the design and use of the assessment

- Empower teachers to trust their own professional judgments about learners

- Nourish trust and cooperation between teachers and students

- Focus on students' strengths rather than just reveal their weaknesses

- Provide information that is used to advocate for students rather than penalize them

- Support meaningful standards based on the understanding that growth and excellence can take many forms

- Are integral parts of instruction

- Gather multiple measures over time and in a variety of meaningful contexts

- Provide educators and others with richer and fairer information about all children, including those who come from linguistically and culturally diverse backgrounds

- Are part of a systemic approach to improving education that includes strengthening the curriculum, professional development for teachers, and additional support for helping those children who need it

- Provide information that is clear and useful to students, teachers, parents, and other stakeholders

- Continually undergo review, revision, and improvement

In this chapter we provide you with helpful strategies and activities that can be aligned with these indicators of authentic and useful assessment practices.

Assessment of Social Competency

The reason we are including social competency before anything else in this section on assessment is that a child who is highly stressed in a learning environment—or who is behaving so badly that he or she interferes consistently with the learning of others—is probably going to make negligible literacy progress. Support for the growth of a child's intrapersonal and interpersonal intelligence is important in and of itself (Gardner, 1993), but it is also critical in terms of the child's literacy potential. After children have been in the classroom for at least a month, an inventory (Figure 5.1) should be taken of their developing social competency, and more active attention should then be focused on helping them move toward increased self-regulation and social competency when needed. Subsequent assessment should occur for children at least twice more during the school year. Instruction designed to build social competency in children should be as carefully planned as that for literacy development so that children are scaffolded toward increasingly productive social behavior. It can often be integrated into our literacy work with children, because there are so many well-written children's narratives about problem solving and positive social interaction with others. Puppets can often be used to get across concepts about more positive social interactions with others. For children with minimal social skills and a marked inability to regulate their own behavior without adult/peer reminders, a referral should be made as early as possible for diagnostic assessment and extra assistance in working with the child and family. The bottom line is that a child who cannot work or play cooperatively, ask for help when necessary, or begin and pursue a task will eventually fall behind. We want to cut off that possibility as early as possible.

If you are in a program that wants to keep a more formal record of children's social skills development for research purposes, we would recommend that you consider two standardized instruments:

1. Devereux Early Childhood Assessment (DECA) (LeBuffe & Naglieri, 1998). Recommended by the NAEYC, the DECA assesses social–emotional

FIGURE 5.1   PK/K Social Competency Assessment

PK/K Social Competency Assessment

Child's Name _____

Competency and Regulation Skills	Date _____ Test Age _____	Date _____ Test Age _____	Date _____ Test Age _____
1. Separates from parent without distress			
2. Verbalizes feelings			
3. Asks for help when necessary			
4. Works and plays cooperatively			
5. Knows how to calm self down			
6. Respects materials and equipment			
7. Respects adults			
8. Waits turn before speaking			
9. Follows rules of classroom and school without reminders			
10. Helps to clean up after activities			
11. Can usually resolve own conflicts			
12. Is friendly and helpful to others			
13. Is liked by other children; attracts friends			
14. Is capable of making good learning choices independently			
15. Follows directions well			
16. Adjusts to changes in routine without undue stress			

FIGURE **5.1** *(Continued)*

Competency and Regulation Skills	Date _____ Test Age _____	Date _____ Test Age _____	Date _____ Test Age _____
17. Comforts or helps others who are upset, hurt, or having difficulty			
18. Can wait his/her turn			
19. Sticks to an activity for as long as can be expected for a child that age			
20. Shares materials, equipment			
21. Accepts new activities without fear or reluctance			
22. Has an adequate amount of energy during the class period			
23. Is eager to participate in classroom activities			
24. Shows self-confidence			
25. Stays on task when necessary; attempts to finish a task			
Total Number of Skills Identified			

development (initiative, self-control, and attachment). It is an observational rating scale (37 items) that can be used in conjunction with a training program: Classroom Strategies for Reducing Behavioral Concerns. A Spanish version is available.

2. Social Competence and Behavior Evaluation (SCBE), Preschool Edition (LaFreniere & Dumas, 1995). This instrument was designed to assess patterns of social competence, affective expression, and adjustment difficulties in children age 30 to 78 months. It is an eighty-item

questionnaire to be completed by a teacher in approximately fifteen minutes. The primary purpose is to describe behavioral tendencies for the purposes of socialization and education, rather than to classify children within diagnostic categories. It allows teachers to orient classroom intervention efforts toward the child's strengths as well as weaknesses. Raw scores and summary scores are obtained.

A General Literacy Skills Checklist

A well-designed curriculum should serve as the basis for determining the literacy outcomes that you are targeting for the school year. Very simply, however, during the year before kindergarten and then again during kindergarten, a child's emerging literacy skills are best concentrated on increased oral language facility and reading and writing concepts and skills. When teachers plan engaging activities for children on a daily basis, and parents contribute with more of these at home, children make almost unbelievable progress during this two-year period. As with social competency assessment, evaluation of a child's literacy skills should be formally documented early in October, again in February, and, finally, at the end of the school year. This should take place via observation by the teacher, through work samples produced by the child, and by direct assessment in miniconferences with the child. A tool to support direct assessment of forty-five literacy skills that should emerge during this time period is presented in Figure 5.2. Three major areas of development are of interest: oral language development (receptive and expressive), writing skills and concepts, and reading and viewing skills and concepts.

For formal assessment of early literacy skills, several standardized instruments that we recommend (and are also recommended by the National Child Care Information Center are the following:

1. *Illinois Snapshots of Early Literacy* (ISEL) (Barr, Blachowicz, Buhle, Chaney, Ivy, & Súarez–Silva, (2002)—According to Teale (2003), the instrument was commissioned by the Illinois State Board of Education to (1) provide assessment information for classroom instructional planning, (2) identify children needing an early reading intervention program, and (3) provide pre- and postassessment data on literacy progress. There are individually administered subtests on alphabet

FIGURE 5.2   PK/K Literacy Skill Checklist

PK/K Literacy Assessment

Child's Name _____

Emerging Literacy Skills	Date _____ Test Age _____	Date _____ Test Age _____	Date _____ Test Age _____
Oral language: Listening and Speaking			
1. Listens attentively to a story			
2. Speaks clearly enough to be understood			
3. Uses complete sentences			
4. Participates in singing, finger plays, movement activity			
5. Attaches sounds to letters			
6. Identifies sets of rhyming words			
7. Has age-appropriate receptive language			
8. Has age-appropriate expressive language			
9. Exhibits increasing comfort and confidence when speaking			
10. Experiments and plays with sounds (rhyming, alliteration, and other aspects of phonological awareness)			
11. In conversation, uses vocabulary words learned from stories and other sources			
12. Is increasing complexity of words and sentences used			
13. Understands the role of participants in conversations			
Writing Skills and Concepts			
14. Has hand control needed to write			

(continues)

FIGURE **5.2** *(Continued)*

Emerging Literacy Skills	Date _____ Test Age _____	Date _____ Test Age _____	Date _____ Test Age _____
15. Writes first name			
16. Writes first and last names			
17. Draws recognizable picture (self, family, objects, events)			
18. Writes ten letters			
19. Understands that ideas can be written and then read by others			
20. Writes 26 letters			
21. Uses a variety of early writing (scribbling, drawing, letter strings, copying environmental print)			
22. Writes about experiences, using phonetic and/or conventional spelling in sentences			
23. Writes two or more connected sentences			
24. Senses need to look over and modify writings and drawings (add to, edit)			
Reading and Viewing Skills and Concepts			
25. Recognizes own name			
26. Identifies letters in first name			
27. Identifies ten letters (of 26 letters randomly displayed)			
28. Recognizes others' names and personally meaningful words			
29. Identifies 26 letters randomly displayed			
30. Understands print and book handling concepts (e.g., front/back, title)			

FIGURE **5.2** *(Continued)*

Emerging Literacy Skills	Date _____ Test Age _____	Date _____ Test Age _____	Date _____ Test Age _____
31. Understands that printed materials have various forms and functions (e.g., signs, labels, notes, menus, letters)			
32. Reads three to five simple sight words			
33. Identifies punctuation (period, question mark, comma, exclamation mark, quotation marks)			
34. Talks about preferences for favorite authors, kinds of books and topics			
35. Identifies an uppercase or capital letter			
36. Points to first/last letter in name			
37. Points to where reader begins reading a story (text)			
38. Points to where reader goes next (sweep)			
39. Retells a story he/she has heard			
40. Understands the role of author and illustrator			
41. Pretends to read a book, pointing to words and telling story			
42. Decodes a variety of print (logographic, individual words, unfamiliar names)			
43. Reads a simple book			
44. Uses different strategies for understanding written material (e.g., predictions, connecting to experiences, past knowledge, asking questions, pictures, structure of text)			
45. Chooses to read, write, listen, speak, and view for enjoyment and information			
Total Number of 45 Skills Identified			

recognition, story listening (comprehension and vocabulary), phonemic awareness, one-to-one matching and word naming, letter sounds, developmental spelling, word recognition, and graded passage reading. Provides both standardized and qualitative data and diagnostic information for classroom-based instruction.

2. *Teacher Rating of Oral Language and Literacy* (TROLL) (Dickinson, McCabe, & Sprague, 2003)—An observational rating scale that rates competence in English and in the child's native language as well (e.g., Does the child recognize his or her own first name in print? No = 1; Yes = 2). This may be downloaded at www.getgotgo.net. The TROLL correlates significantly with scores on the Peabody Picture Vocabulary Test and Early Phonemic Awareness Profile. There are 25 items, and the tool takes five to ten minutes to administer.

3. *Head Start—National Reporting System* (NRS)—Designed for four- and five-year-olds; evaluates the following:

   a. Understanding and using language to communicate for various purposes

   b. Using increasingly complex and varied vocabulary

   c. In the case of children whose native language is other than English, progressing toward acquisition of the English language

   d. Identifying at least ten letters of the alphabet

   e. Acquiring numeracy awareness

4. *Phonological Awareness Literacy Screening*—Phonological awareness and literacy screening tool that measures literacy knowledge predictive of future reading success: awareness of rhyme and beginning sounds, ability to name letters of the alphabet (uppercase and lowercase), familiarity with books and print (identifying concepts of print and interacting with print in a real reading context), and name writing. Strengths are identified as well as areas that require additional support.

5. *Preschool Language Scale*—Measures both receptive and expressive language skills in children three to seven years of age. Takes fifteen to forty-five minutes to administer. Raw and derivative scores, including age equivalents, standard deviations to determine risk are provided.

Children naturally vary in the speed at which these literacy skills develop. As pointed out earlier, chronological, experiential, and gender differences in preprimary and kindergarten children contribute to these variances. However, for children who make slow progress, assessment should occur more often. Again, when lags are considerable, referrals should be made for diagnostic evaluation. Assessment should always lead directly to instruction that addresses skill and concept building in groups of children or for individual children who are ahead or behind the group. Otherwise, there is no good reason to do assessments.

Screening and Assessment of Young English Language Learners

Today, there are an estimated 45 million U.S. school-age children. Of these, more than one in five live in households in which the primary language is not English (Winzer & Mazurek, 1998). The greatest number of these children are Spanish speaking and of Hispanic descent. Previously located just in the American southwest, there has been a literal recent explosion in the number of Hispanics in the entire United States, and this number is expected to grow significantly. Many of the children grow up in homes in which parents may be monolingual, speaking only Spanish, or bilingual. Of the latter group, parents may code switch, alternating between English and Spanish.

Assessment of young second language learners is not easy in general, because language assessment leans so heavily on a child's language capability. The first step in assessing growth and capability in young second language learners is deciding what you need to know about. Tabors (1997) underscores the importance of the following:

1. The child's cognitive, social–emotional, and physical development

2. The child's capability with his or her first language

3. The child's capabilities with a second or additional language

4. The abilities that the child demonstrates nonverbally

In our everyday interactions with English language learners, there are some observations we can make strategically to determine whether they (and other children as well) are developing language facility in their interactions with others: Carol Seefeldt (2005, 91) outlines the following:

■ Note how children are moving from incomplete to more complete sentences as they talk about their experiences.

■ Notice whether individual children are able to express their preferences of what to do when playing.

■ Record when and how children name equipment and objects.

■ Note children's use of verbs to describe their actions and the actions of others.

■ Listen to children discuss their drawings. Note how individual children are becoming more articulate and able (and willing) to express themselves in front of the group.

■ Note how children respond to stories. Are they attentive? Record any questions they ask, predictions they make, and whether they are able to relate the story to their own experiences.

■ Ask individual children to tell what they like to do best. Note and record nouns and verbs they use.

■ Keep dated samples of any writing the children do. Look at use of **invented spelling,** numbers of correct letters used, correct syllabification, and use of conventional spelling.

Lopez, Salas, and Flores (2005, 48–52) suggest that assessment of children who are English language learners must also go beyond developing language concerns to be nondiscriminatory. Consideration of other factors in the child's life, such as acculturation, the role of language, and family participation must be evaluated. They suggest interview questions that might be helpful to use with parents to examine acculturation and language usage and preference:

■ How many years have you lived in the United States? What about your child?

■ How do you identify yourself ethnically? How would you identify your child?

■ What types of television programs does your child watch?

■ Do you read to your child? In what languages do you read to your child?

■ With whom do you and your children spend the most time?

- Do you interact with a particular family member?

- How much time do you spend together?

- What language does your child use in the home?

- What language does the child use with friends, relatives, and others?

- Does the child alternate between two languages?

- When with a primary caregiver, in what language does the child choose to communicate?

- In what language is the child given guidance/discipline?

- If your child was born in the United States, to what extent has he or she been exposed to English?

One of the things that we need to be very careful about in assessing the English language learner in English is that tests that require higher order thinking skills—analysis, synthesis, evaluation, generalization, conclusion formulation, and so forth—are highly inappropriate for use with children who have had less than five to seven years to acquire cognitive academic language proficiency (Cummins, 1981; Hernandez, 1989). Heather Biggar (2005, 44–51) has indicated that assessing young children whose first language is not English requires skill, sensitivity, and knowledge of a child's culture and primary language. She notes that despite the rapid growth of young English language learners in the United States, the field currently lacks appropriate tools to assess their skills, professional development for teachers to build effective strategies to support the children, community and political awareness of need, and financial resources to address needs. She makes seven recommendations that stakeholders can use to develop or refine policy and practices in assessment of English language learners:

1. Use screening and assessment for appropriate, specific, and beneficial purposes only, and adapt them to meet the needs of children whose home language is not English.

2. Use culturally and linguistically appropriate assessments.

3. Use characteristics of assessment to improve instruction, learning, and development, and maximize teachers' curriculum planning and teaching strategies.

4. Use standardized formal assessments and state tests only when the development and interpretation of the assessments take into consideration issues related to English language learners.

Useful and Authentic Assessment Strategies

5. Ensure that those conducting assessments of English language learners have cultural and linguistic competence, knowledge of the child being assessed, and specific assessment-related knowledge and skills.

6. Involve the families of English language learners in the assessment process in a variety of appropriate ways (e.g., see the discussion later in this chapter on student-led conferencing).

7. Work to ensure rapid progress in meeting particular assessment needs in the field—in other words, expanding the knowledge base; developing more and better assessments; increasing the number of bilingual and bicultural professionals; and creating professional development opportunities for administrators, supervisors, practitioners, and other stakeholders in effective assessment of young English language learners.

Observation and Anecdotal Notation

Taking time to become a "kidwatcher" is absolutely the most effective assessment strategy you have available for documenting children's increasing concepts and skills relative to emerging literacy. To do this effectively, you have to have internalized a good store of knowledge about what young children are capable of learning during preschool and kindergarten years. You must also be very certain about the outcomes you want during the school year. What skills do you want all the children to have when they leave your classroom in the spring?

After you have identified *observable* outcomes, the next step is to take time to watch and record behavior in the children that shows evidence of or lack of growth. All teachers have time to do this if they have children working independently or at centers for at least an hour a day. Let's look at this a little more closely: If, for example, you have 25 children in your classroom, one fifth of the children can be selected for observation on Monday, one-fifth on Tuesday, and so on. The next week, groups of children should be rotated to another day so that certain children are not always watched on Monday or Friday, for example. You will want to keep a clipboard handy, with an observation grid form (Figure 5.3) on which there is room to record each child's name and a place to make brief notes. You may also record your observations on sticky notes that can be put right into a child's individual folder. Brief mini conferences can be conducted

FIGURE **5.3**   Observation Grid

Observation Grid

Date: _____

Monday	Tuesday	Wednesday	Thursday	Friday

during this time to assess whether a child is increasing a skill (e.g., able to name ten letters out of 26 randomly displayed letters). At the end of the day, you will want to take five minutes to record any additional thoughts about these five children. A lot can be written in one minute of concentrated time in thinking about a child. When this kind of practice takes place, a teacher who teaches 36 weeks a year will have 36 day-long observations about each child in the classroom. This provides in-depth knowledge of all children in the classroom and important information for designing classroom activity and sharing information with parents. More important, you will find yourself paying more attention to each and every child in your classroom, rather than just to those who are more active, aggressive, or challenging.

The Ecomap

Children's lives outside the classroom heavily influence their in-school performance. For example, the child who has adequate family stability, nutrition, health care, rest, and diverse learning experiences will be in better shape in the classroom than the child who does not. Learning more about who lives in the household, the child's extracurricular involvement, whether there are family pets, who neighborhood friends are, and other aspects of a child's world outside the classroom are all helpful for building rapport with the child inside the classroom. During a home visit or fall conference, an ecomap (Figure 5.4) can be used to glean all kinds of helpful information. Using the form, a teacher can comfortably interview a parent about all the connections a child has in which he or she spends time away from the classroom, as well as the important people in a child's life. Critical events in the child's life can be recorded, including such happenings as an accident, chronic illness or hospitalization, separation or divorce of parents, death of a valued grandparent, birth of a sibling, and other meaningful occurrences. This is not intended as a means for being "nosy"; rather, it is intended as a means of sharing information between adults who will be partnered for the year in advancing the child's overall development. After teachers present the ecomap concept in this way, the child's parents or caregivers are often eager to identify a variety of ecomap components and construct their own copy during the discussion. One teacher also uses this information to help her make selections of narrative picture books to read to the children and have available in the classroom.

FIGURE **5.4**   Updated Ecomap for Alvin, Age 5 years and 2 months

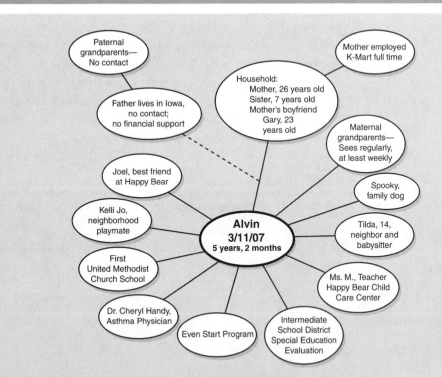

Critical events learned through interviews with mother on 9/18/06 and 3/11/07:

1/19/2002	Birth in Ames, Iowa. Birth weight = 4.3. Hospitalized for first four weeks in neonatal intensive care unit.
5/2003	Moves with mother to Illinois. Parents separate, and father remains in Iowa.
8/2003	Mother returns to work force. Alvin is enrolled in a local day care center, attending 7:30 a.m. to 6:00 p.m.
2/2004	Parents divorce. Chronic ear infections and asthma. No child custody paid.
6/2004	Change in day care. Enrolled in new center. Teacher advises assessment for hearing impairment and language delay. Tubes subsequently put in ears. Thirty-four days absent because of asthma-related illness.
11/2004	Hospitalized for tonsillectomy.
6/2005	Family identified as eligible for Even Start Program. Mother enrolls.
9/6/06	Alvin enrolled in public school preschool program.
9/18/06	Teacher makes home visit. First ecomap completed.
11/06	Alvin out of school two weeks because of asthma.
1/07	Alvin returns to Iowa for visit with paternal grandparents. Out of school for one week.
2/12/07	Teacher requests home visit to discuss behavior issues.
3/11/07	Parent/teacher conference. Forty-eight days absent because of illness during school year so far and other reasons. Ecomap update completed.

Child Self-Appraisal

The onus on learning should be shared by the child. Children gain a great deal when they understand that they also bear responsibility for their own learning in the classroom. Helping them organize their thinking about what skills they need to accomplish is the first step. This can be done by providing a form for them that lists five to ten *observable* emerging literacy skills and having them date and check it every week or month in a brief mini conference with you (Figure 5.5). Nothing that is not directly observable should go on such a form.

FIGURE **5.5**   Sample Child Self-Check List

Look, I can do these things!

Literacy Skills	Oct.	Nov.	Dec.	Jan.	Feb.	Mar.	Apr.	May
I can recognize my name.								
I can write my first name.								
I can name the letters in my first name.								
I can tell a nursery rhyme I know.								
I can draw a picture of myself.								
I can write my first and last names.								
I can point to where you start reading a story.								
I can recognize the names of two friends.								
I can identify ten alphabet letters.								
I can write all 26 of the alphabet letters.								

If children cannot do a particular skill but insist on coloring it in or checking the form, you'll want to explain that the skill needs to be demonstrated first before being checked, and allow the child to do so. Work samples the child has produced can be used. At the end of the activity, again verbalize what's still on the list (and what's already been accomplished!) and ask the child, "What do you think you want to work on for the next time we sit down with this list?" Prior to the next assessment, remind the child occasionally of the targeted skill being worked on, provide scaffolded support so the child can progress toward the skill, and provide genuine praise and encouragement any time the child attempts to make progress or master the skill.

When an entire checklist has been completed by the child, a check-list with a new list of skills, based on the literacy curriculum, should be developed. However, you should always want to include at least one or two skills the child can already do and others that the child can reason-ably accomplish with assistance and effort.

Children's Performance Samples

Having a child demonstrate a skill (e.g., "Write as many words as you know." "Show me the letters that you know and tell me their names." "Tell me a word that rhymes with pan.") is the best way to determine whether the child is building a repertoire of literacy skills. Noting what the skill is, the child's performance, and dating the sample for future reference and comparison is one way to document growth. Children may also produce drawings and/or written work that can be dated and later compared. The following are several assessments that we think are useful and appropriate for older preschoolers and kindergarten children. They can be completed in October, February, and May to assess the child's growing ability to think of words and spell them. We look also at the child's growing sophistication in their ability to depict detail in the related drawings.

Nursery Rhyme Repetition

As an assessment procedure, model reading a familiar nursery rhyme (see Figures 5.6 and 5.7) from a class chart over and over until children are familiar with it (e.g., Jack and Jill). Then model writing it several times, having children give you some letters whenever possible. After establishing familiarity, have the children draw a picture portraying

Jack and Jill, and then have them attempt to write the rhyme themselves, not looking at the stimulus. The youngest or least experienced children may only be able to make undecipherable marks at the beginning. As their recognition of details, and letter–sound and letter–grapheme associations grows, you will see growth reflected in the follow-up assessments. Assess the children in October, February, and May, using the same rhyme stimulus to standardize the process and modeling the procedure in a large or small group before asking

FIGURE **5.6**   Three Handwriting Samples of a Nursery Rhyme Repetition

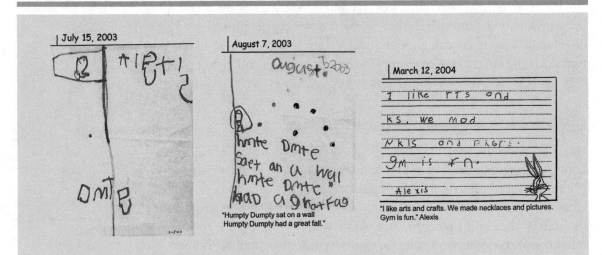

"Humpty Dumpty sat on a wall
Humpty Dumpty had a great fall."

"I like arts and crafts. We made necklaces and pictures. Gym is fun." Alexis

FIGURE **5.7**   Nursery Rhyme Repetition

children to do the task individually. Frequently use other nursery rhymes at other times during the year, sharing the pen with the children so that they become very familiar with the task.

Attribute Naming

One of the skills we're interested in seeing grow during the year is for children to be able to think of vocabulary words that are descriptive and to be able to grow in their ability to spell the words conventionally. Attribute naming (Soderman, et al., 2005) is one of those activities that children love to do in a small or large group that enhances both skills. In a large group, place a familiar picture in the middle of the easel (e.g., Curious George). Have the children provide words related to Curious George (e.g., tail, mouth, eyes, arms, ears, bicycle), which you will write, again having the children help with the spelling whenever possible. Then, provide the children with a sheet of paper with a picture of Curious George in the middle and remove the large-group model that has been completed. Have them work independently or in pairs to write as many words as they can related to Curious George, using invented spelling. This is a good "test" to evaluate increasing fluidity (number of words they can write each time) and also increased ability to spell conventionally (number of words spelled correctly). Use the same stimulus in October, February, and May to standardize the process; however, this exercise can be done weekly with many other stimuli (e.g., a dog, a fish, a baby, a house, a car) that would allow children to think of related words.

Self-Portraits

Just as in writing, drawing becomes more sophisticated as children begin to notice details, direction, size, shape, and differences in abstract figures, and gain both the physical dexterity and memory they need to represent what is in their head. It is worthwhile to have children draw self-portraits (Figure 5.8) at several junctures throughout the year and label their body parts if they are able, to determine whether there is growth in the skill needed to do this. One teacher we know obtains a baseline figure at the beginning of the year, dates it, and stores it for future comparisons. He then spends time with the children, having them become more observant about what the human face looks like— their own and their classmates'. He asks the children to study one

FIGURE **5.8**

Kindergarten Self-
Portraits

another's faces, looking at how eyes, noses, and mouths are shaped; where ears are connected; and the presence of eyelashes, eyebrows, freckles, and other adornments. He also provides mirrors, has children cut out pictures of faces from magazines, and has them identify and label sad, angry, happy, excited, surprised, and other emotions in the faces they are selecting. The time he spends on this kind of activity pays off in the children's ability to fill in greater detail on their own faces when they are drawing self-portraits. He follows this later with the same kind of attention on bodies: How are they hinged? What are "appendages?" Where on the body are they connected? What can bodies do? How are bodies shaped differently? These activities contribute to children's abilities in other areas, including assessment, because they become more skilled in visual observation and ability to represent their reflections on paper. When their work samples are dated, they become excellent tools for comparison and documentation of growth.

Classroom Assessment That Promotes Learning

Jay McTighe and Ken O'Connor (2005) maintain that classroom assessment has the potential not only to measure and document learning, but to promote it. They suggest seven practices:

1. *Use summative assessments to frame meaningful performance goals.* You do this, for example, when you provide the children in your classroom with a literacy self-appraisal checklist, going through the checklist with them periodically and saying, "Remember, these are skills that I want you to work on with my help. Every week, we will sit down together to see if you've been able to learn how to do one or more of these. If you can, you'll be able to color in or check off the skill. It'll be exciting when you can check off all ten or five of these. We'll work on these together."

2. *Show criteria and models in advance.* You do this when you are doing activities such as attribute naming or nursery rhyme repetition in small and large groups. You demonstrate how to do the activity and then remove the stimulus and allow the children to do it by themselves. You do this, as well, when you model in large or small groups such activities as sorting words that begin with the certain letters (e.g., A, S, and T) and then allow individual children or pairs of children to replicate the activity, observing and noting their performance. Preschool and kindergarten teachers are very good at providing "previews of coming attractions" to young children who work in centers. It also works for natural assessment activities that just become part of the everyday classroom work.

3. *Assess before teaching.* Gaining baseline knowledge of what children know and what they *want* to know is important in terms of shaping good instruction. When preschool and kindergarten children come in, they vary dramatically in terms of their experience and what they know about letters, words, stories, colors, shapes, concepts, and ideas. McTighe and O'Connor (2005) provide an example of baseline and follow-up assessment:

> Before beginning instruction on the five senses, a kindergarten teacher asks each student to draw a picture of the body parts related to the various senses and show what each part does. She models the process by drawing an eye on the chalkboard. "The eye helps us see things around us," she points out. As students draw, the teacher circulates around the room, stopping to ask clarifying questions ("I see you've drawn a nose. What does the nose help us do?"). On the basis of what she learns about her students from this diagnostic pretest, she divides the class into two groups for differentiated instruction. At the conclusion of the unit, the teacher asks students to do another drawing,

which she collects and compares with their original pretest as evidence of their learning. (14)

Teachers have a number of ways to find out what very young children know before they launch into new units of study. They can read a related book to children and then have a guided conversation with them about the content. They can develop concept maps with the children, ranging out in lots of different directions to evaluate experience and knowledge. They can ask directly about knowledge and what children understand or misunderstand about a phenomenon by using a KWL activity (What do you *know?* What do you *want* to know? What did we *learn?*).

4. *Offer appropriate choices.* If we buy into the power of the Reggio Emelia belief that children have a "hundred languages" to represent the ideas and skills they have, we will also be able to buy into the legitimacy of offering children choices in demonstrating what they know. Let's take an assessment of children's growing sight word recognition, for example. One child or group of children may enjoy an activity of moving about the classroom to read the many familiar labels that have been placed on objects and equipment. Another child or group of children may enjoy reading the words on the word wall. Still another child may enjoy going through the class-made dictionary at the writing center, naming the words that have been listed.

5. *Provide feedback early and often.* Earlier we suggested that you spend time observing children and making notations about what you see. This is a time when you can provide brief, helpful assistance and feedback to one or more children: "I see you're writing a lot of words. What do you think you could do to remember to put spaces between them?" "You think the first thing that happened in the story is that the flea bit the mouse. Here's a copy of the book. Let's go back and check it out." "You think Marciella's name has an 'h' in it. Let's go over to the word wall and check that out." Making sure that children have at least an hour a day to work at well-designed and interesting centers frees you up to find out what children know, and to provide the feedback and encouragement they need on a daily basis from you as they build new levels of understanding.

6. *Encourage self-assessment and goal setting.* We've discussed the value of a child's self-appraisal. Teachers can create any number of

child-friendly and engaging checklists of skills the children are attempting to achieve. These should be attractive, easy for the children to understand in terms of the responses they are to provide, and related to the work they are doing every day in the early childhood classroom. Having children involved in the initial listing of the skills (with the teacher's guidance about what fits) is important whenever possible, and teachers will want to keep children directed toward the goal: "It's hard at first to write all the letters in our names, but when we sign in every day, using our name tags for help, we're getting better and better at it, aren't we?"

7. *Allow new evidence of achievement to replace old evidence.* This is where the **portfolio** collections (described next) come in handy. One child, looking at a drawing he had made of his family early in the year and another made at the end of the year, referred to the first one and laughed, "I was such a baby then!" There is not a better method than dating and saving samples of children's work for visibly demonstrating the considerable growth a child makes during the course of several months or a year. At the same time, we build earned pride in the child and the recognition that effort pays off.

Portfolios and Student-Led Conferencing

What if you could find a way to keep track of the many levels of learning that go on in your classroom that would help children become more analytical about their own learning? What if you had a foolproof method for teaching them to set reachable goals, organize their work, increase their self-confidence, and give them an ability to take on more responsibility on a day-to-day basis? What if this practice actually made your teaching and their learning more fun? Would you be interested?

Your first response might be that with all you're currently expected to do, you can't pile one more thing into your week-to-week teaching. You might think that the children you teach are too young, not skillful enough, or not responsible enough to pull off something like this. You might worry that you would have to give up teaching practices you've come to enjoy over the years, be required to throw everything away, and learn a completely different way of teaching children. Not so!

We'd like to share with you the power of portfolios and student-led conferencing as a comprehensive assessment method that can help you put more of the onus for learning on children, develop more independent and engaged learners, and get parents more involved in the learning process. The only thing you would have to throw away is the image of yourself as the only one in control of the learning that goes on in your classroom this year. You will discover how to enjoy sharing that with the learners.

You may have a portfolio somewhere at home that you've never called a portfolio. It may contain papers you wrote while in elementary, high school, or college that you were particularly proud of (we save only our very best, of course!). There may be certificates or awards received, professional degrees granted, before-and-after pictures of a project you worked on alone or with others, or evidence of committees on which you were active. It may contain pictures of friends or family taken during memorable events. It is a collection that represents your personal achievement and growth—and it feels good to go through it from time to time.

The classroom that best facilitates the use of portfolios is one that children and teachers are reluctant to leave at the end of the year. It is one that has become a solid learning community where real work is valued, accomplished, and documented. It is clearly one where life skills are fostered and where children come to understand how, with real effort on their part over time, they are becoming more skilled and more knowledgeable about a whole bevy of things. This approach to assessment and evaluation provides new insights for teachers, and it empowers and motivates children to give greater value to their work and to the processes involved in their learning. It also fosters creativity, respects each child's individuality, creates independent work habits, and improves children's self-esteem (Soderman et al., 2005).

Kinds of Porfolios

Portfolios take many forms. Artists, models, photographers, and businesses often organize unique collections that represent the best of what they have done over a period of time. As children progress through school, they can build collections of their best work, too. The following pages note several forms of portfolios that you may want to consider:

Working Portfolio. This is a file the children keep of selected samples of everyday work. Some teachers feel parents will be disappointed if the child does not bring home something every day to decorate the refrigerator. You will want to share with parents at the beginning of the year that some days you will be asking children to save their work in a folder, which they will then share with them on a special day. After deciding what kinds of samples you want children to save for their portfolios, there will be certain days when you will tell children ahead of time, "Today, we will want to keep our self-portraits (or self-appraisal checklist or word family list) in our portfolios so we can show them to our families on a special day." These individual working portfolios should be placed in an area of the room that is readily accessible. Typically, the working portfolio is just a manila folder that is labeled and decorated by the child. It can be kept in a hanging file with other children's folders. The children's picture can be used as a tab so that they can readily find their own file. Special wooden carts to house portfolio hanging files, which take up very little space, are available at teacher supply stores. Send the contents of the working portfolio home periodically, after selecting items for the showcase portfolio discussed next.

Showcase Portfolio. This form of portfolio is what allows children to become reflective and selective about the work they have done during a specific period. It should communicate to parents the amount of growth that has taken place from one time to another, and should contain several dated samples of the child's best work.

Prior to the student-led conference (discussed later), you will want to have children take four or five of their favorite pieces from the working portfolio. During center time, draw out one child at a time to do this and encourage the child to tell you why the particular pieces have been chosen. To help children articulate why a piece is valuable, you can add your own comments: "I'm glad you chose that piece. It's one of my favorites, too, because it's the first time I saw you leaving spaces between your words." Children can decorate a special folder in which to place these pieces in preparation for a visit from their families or other friends.

Teacher Portfolio. You will want to keep a separate manila folder for each child in your classroom; no doubt, you already do this. These folders are often housed in a milk crate or file cabinet and should contain checklists, anecdotal notes you've taken about the child from observations you've made, health alerts, copies of the child's work that you believe are representative of something you want to discuss with a parent or other professional, communications to and from parents or other stakeholders, and anything else you believe is important in terms of record keeping about that particular child. This portfolio can also contain information sent forward from previous teachers, such as an ecomap.

Institutional Portfolio. If you are planning to implement portfolios, we are hoping every other teacher in your school will cooperate with you to collect certain information each year about every child.

The amount and kind of information should be thoughtfully defined, and nothing should go into the institutional portfolio except what has been agreed to by everyone. That way, the collection does not get to be unwieldy. If used as a teacher portfolio during the school year, it should be cleaned out at the end of the year, with everything removed that is extraneous. This portfolio should then go back to the school office to be redistributed the following year to the child's new teacher. If the child moves during or after the school year, it is helpful to have the portfolio mailed to the child's forwarding school. When saved over the entire preschool and elementary years, these folders can become part of a "graduation" celebration for every child at the end of his or her time at a particular school. The portfolios should be cleared of any information that does not represent the child's best work and presented to the child and his or her family during a special evening. Children and their parents are thrilled to receive a collection of work that's been produced over a number of years.

Class Portfolios. Class portfolios are "extra," but can serve the important purpose of unifying a class into a community of learners and documenting collaborative work, friendships that grow over the year, and group accomplishments. A class portfolio may take the form of a cumulative video, showing children working at particular tasks, putting on such events as readers' theater or a play, reciting poetry, setting off a class-constructed volcano, or singing a song they've created. The video may be set up so that it runs continually during student-led conferences in the classroom or hallway where all parents and children may view it together before or after their visit in the classroom.

Documentation boards, loaded with pictures taken during a period of several weeks or focused on particular projects from beginning to end can also be created, using a digital camera to keep costs low. Inexpensive three-sided boards can be purchased at office supply shops. Children can dictate or write about objectives for the work depicted, and teachers can put brief narrative comments by each picture about what they meant to have children learning at that point in time.

Bulletin boards inside and outside the classroom, as well as class books and scrapbooks (which children love to look through over and over) can also become repositories for documentation of class work over the year. The value of these class portfolios is to keep the excitement of goal accomplishment in front of teachers, children, and their parents throughout the year.

What Can Portfolios Contain?   We've already given a few hints of items that can be included in children's portfolios. You will want to include both examples of the learning process and finished products. Examples include student self-appraisal forms, baseline and follow-up work samples, drawings and artwork, self- and family portraits completed months apart and dated, photographs of products produced, photos of friends, story maps, books made, and journal entries. These are only some ideas of what others have chosen to include. You will have your own ideas about this—and so will your children!

Getting Started.   Now for the exciting part—actually putting this into practice with the children! You've already thought about the kinds of work performance samples you can have children save. The next step is to acquaint children with what portfolios are all about and your excitement for involving them in such a process. You can share a portfolio of your own that you've made for just that purpose, helping children to understand the value of the collection to the owner and how it tells a story about what the owner has accomplished.

Show them where they will be storing the work they are producing for the portfolio. Underscore how important it is to put their work in the folder in an organized and careful way. Explain that this will not be a place to keep papers, but a place to put *specific* work so they can watch how they are learning to be readers and writers at school. Let them know that you believe they are responsible enough to begin this process and that you will help them with reminders about work to put in this special folder.

Provide a folder for each child. Brainstorm ways they can decorate, individualize, and title their covers. A comfortable and fun first entry can be a self-portrait. Help them date the completed piece and place it in the folder. At this time, have them look over other personal work samples they may have hanging in the room and add another piece to the portfolio. Tell them that they will be adding to their portfolios every week, and share some of the possible items they can include, saying, "We don't have to add all these right away. We'll have plenty of time to add items, and you'll think of some yourself that you want to save." Remind them that work for their portfolios should always reflect their best effort and most careful work.

Finally, don't take over! Resist the urge to take complete control. If you do, children don't have the opportunity to develop responsibility. On the other hand, you will have to provide lots of support to these very young children who are just beginning to learn about portfolio collections. Don't give up easily. The benefits of keeping portfolios and holding student-led conferences are too great to abandon them without a supreme effort.

Planning for the Celebration, Student-Led Conferencing

When we teach, according to Fox (1997, 128), we need celebrations—to amaze children with their own capabilities; to create a willingness to continue learning; to lift the spirits, renew ambition, and set new goals. Student-led conferences can be those kinds of celebrations (Figure 5.9).

Student-led conferencing calls for teachers to think differently about the way they've always done conferences. This is the tough part. Some teachers are extremely uncomfortable replacing the traditional parent–teacher conference (from which the learner has been almost always excluded) and believe that children, and particularly young

FIGURE **5.9**

Sample Invitation
to a Student-Led
Conference

children, are unable to present their work in a way that really allows parents to see their progress. Other teachers believe that parents only want to hear from the teacher about how their child is doing in relation to the rest of the class (Should we really *ever* do that?), what their child could do to improve, and whether the child is making adequate progress. Our honest response is that if children are experiencing diffi-culty or lagging significantly behind their peers, parents should have been called in for a conference earlier with the teacher. This would call for a longer discussion time than is usually allowed for in traditional conferences. Still other teachers believe that parents will not show up at a conference or prefer just to receive a report card. Our experience with student-led conferencing is that in schools where there has been poor attendance for traditional conferences, almost all parents show up at student-led conferences and report enthusiastically about their experi-ence. When they have had a chance to view their child's work in a relaxed, welcoming atmosphere, accompanied by a child who is proud of the work he or she has produced, parents wouldn't have it any other way. Student-led conferences are especially beneficial for parents and children who speak English as a second language. They have built-in interpreters! For teachers who have viewed student-led conferences with trepidation but have been successful in implementation (everyone is successful!), they wouldn't have it any other way. Preparation is the key to a no-fail plan!

Preparing the Children. After a determined period of time, the children should be invited to select four or five of their favorite pieces from their portfolios to showcase in a student-led conference with their families. This is when their collection becomes a selection and then, when the child learns to explain why they chose a particular piece ("Cause I drawed better in this one."), a reflection relative to the growth they have made. Children can practice showing these pieces to other children in the classroom (one-on-one), to children in another classroom, or to the principal, bus driver, school secretary, or custodian. The big party is yet to come with their families!

Implementing Student-Led Conferences. Children take a great deal of pride in the work they produce in the classroom when they know they will be showcasing it to others later on. Families come in record numbers (usually 100 percent) to student-led conferences, which are enjoyed by everyone. The showcase portfolio discussed previously is prepared. The children think about several activities that are fun to do (e.g., making their name out of clay, making a self-portrait) that their parents might also enjoy doing. In this way, learning that takes place in the classroom, but not exhibited in a portfolio, is also shared with parents. Children practice introducing one another to their teacher, something they will be expected to do with their family members on the special night. They learn that their responsibilities for the evening will be to introduce their family members to the teacher, to take the family members around the room to participate in the planned activities, and to show their portfolio to the family members. A conference organizer to help parents and child "negotiate" the room together can be shared with parents as they enter the room (Figure 5.10).

Preparing the Parents. Parents can be notified during the fall orientation that student-led conferencing will be taking place in February and/or April. The dates should be put on the school's calendar, and parents need to be reminded again in the spring of the upcoming conference. A letter can be sent home to parents one month before the event, letting them know how the conference will be different from traditional conferences and telling them how important it is to have someone from the family attend. An RSVP slip should be included in the letter, so that the

Our Conference Organizer

My child showed me where to sign in on the guest sheet.

My child introduced me to his/her teacher.

We played the bag puppet story together, each of us taking on a different role.

We read the word wall together, alternating words.

We reviewed my/our child's portfolio together.

My child and I enjoyed a snack together.

Together, my child and I completed the conference evaluation.

FIGURE **5.10**

Our Conference
Organizer

teacher can plan for the number of families that will be attending. Also included in the letter to parents may be a few sample questions or comments to use during the conference with their child. Invitations prepared by the children can be sent home a week prior to the event to remind parents again about the evening.

Some teachers prefer to have only one family in the room at a time. However, most plan to have about four families in the room at once, for about 20 to 30 minutes, creating a more partylike atmosphere. Children enjoy it if the other families who are scheduled at the same time are those of their classroom friends, and this is a good way for parents to get to know other families.

If you find that a parent will not be able to attend the conference, be sure to arrange for another adult to accompany the child for the evening. This could be a special invitation to a grandparent, a special education teacher, a school counselor, the principal, a custodian, a secretary, or a teacher aide. The important thing is to make sure someone is there to focus on this child's efforts and achievements for the evening.

Preparing the Room. If you were planning a party at your home, think about what might be on your preparation list. You'd probably do a little extra cleaning or straightening up ahead of your guests arriving, and think about food, music, and maybe some fresh flowers. Getting the children involved in these advance preparations is another good learning experience for them. Have them think about all these things, with guidance from you. On the day before the conferences, time should be allotted to having the children take part in making the room a bit cleaner and neater, choosing some music that will provide a nice background but not interfere with conversation, designing some table covers and decorating them with markers, placing some flowers (or greens gathered from the school yard) on the tables, and preparing

some simple refreshments. The refreshments need not be expensive, but this is one time that parents should not be asked to bring cookies! They should just come and enjoy themselves with their children.

Activities can be set up in the room for children to interact with their parents. For example, centers can be made available for math games or activities. The word wall can be read. Big books and little books can be made available so that parent and child can do some interactive reading. Journals can be set out for children to share. A group project or mini museum can be displayed so that the child can explain the process that took place and his or her part in the project. Portfolios can be placed in a particular center, and it is important that you stress that the child must take adequate time with his or her parents to view and discuss their work. Now, relax. Be a friendly host, along with the children, and see how much more enjoyable this kind of conference is. We promise you'll be thrilled!

Debriefing: What Did Children, Teachers, and Parents Think about the Process?
Debriefing is an important part of student-led conferences. Teachers need to find out how parents and children experienced the event, and to reflect for themselves about what went well and what might be changed the next time around.

Parents can be asked to complete a brief evaluation of the process before they leave for the evening and to place the form in a drop box so their anonymity is protected. Some questions that might be included are

What did you like most about the conference?

What could be improved?

Would you like to see this type of conference format continued in the future? Why or why not?

How do you think your child felt about this kind of conference?

If other teachers in your building were involved in implementing the portfolio and student-led conference processes, get together with them as soon as possible to ask the following questions:

What did we like best about this kind of conference format?

What is gained or lost when implementing this format versus a more traditional parent–teacher conference?

What did the children gain from the experience?

What can be learned from parents' responses to the process?

Would we be in favor of continuing to implement portfolios and student-led conferences? Why or why not?

Even very young children can participate in the evaluation. Have children use the student-led conferences as part of their literacy work the next day. You might create a predictable chart titled "What We Liked about Our Student-Led Conferences" (Figure 5.11).

Parents' comments at these events have included the following:

"I was very proud of how my son was able to show me his work. He was proud, too."

"As small as Cherise is, she seemed to be in touch with her progress so far in school."

"My child was very excited and eager, couldn't wait for tonight. This kind of conference gives kids an understanding of what work is and also pride."

"I didn't know my daughter could be so grown up. She didn't miss a step. It was obvious that she had practiced a lot."

"It gives the kids something to look forward to. The more they learn to do, the more they can show their parents. My child was very proud."

"Overall, it was very smooth. I liked how it made my child responsible and knowing it was important for us both to be there."

What We Liked about Our Student-Led Conferences

I liked the cookies. (Matt)

I liked showing my parents my room. (C. J.)

I liked my dad to see our family picture I drew. (Dequerius)

I liked washing the tables to get ready. (Kara)

I liked seeing my friends. (Kevin)

I liked how my mom saw the stuff I did at the beginning of the year and now. (Janna)

FIGURE 5.11

Simple Predictable
Chart

"I would like very much to see this continue. My child gained a lot, just knowing we care about her education and performance at school."

Teacher's comments have included:

"We had much better attendance with student-led conferences. It would be as if the parents were to miss their child's school play if they didn't show up!"

"Loved it! It was fun and instructive watching the children interact with their parents."

"I was very impressed—and surprised—that my children could be that articulate about what they know . . . very impressed."

"It's much more relaxing. At the same time, parents and students were excited."

"I loved the excitement on the parents' faces on seeing their child's work."

"Everything was gained, and nothing was lost. Parents and children thought it was great. The students took pride in being the one in charge."

We hope this description of portfolios and student-led conferencing has been helpful and that if it has not been a part of your teaching, you'll give it a try this year. The best way is to just dive in and do it.

As can be seen from the previous comments, results are usually very positive. Even very young children win because they become more accountable for their learning and take more ownership. Children clearly make gains in terms of enhanced life skills and independence.

Parents become more active participants in their child's learning. They understand this learning better, and feel that student-led conferences offer a less intimidating and more relaxed atmosphere at the school. At the same time, they walk away with a better understanding of how their child has grown, what kinds of learning activities have promoted that growth, and how their child is feeling about his or her own progress. Student-led conferences create a forum for parents to talk about their child in a positive and productive way.

Schools that have implemented the process, more often than not, conclude that portfolios and student-led conferencing increase the pride children take in their learning, increase parent involvement in the evaluation process, and vastly improve communication between home and school.

Glossary

Academic standards refers to the quality of the systems delivering education, the quality of teachers and their preparation, and the quality of curriculum content and its assessment (Seefeldt, 2005)

Alliteration series of two or more words that begin with the same sound (e.g., Allie ate an apple.)

Alphabetic principle understanding the way that sounds match with letters

Assessment nonformal or standardized tools and methods for measuring children's abilities and skills

Automaticity ability to recognize words encountered in text instantly, without having to decode them deliberately

Comprehension ability to make meaning from the spoken or written word

Concepts of print understanding about the functions (practical uses) structure (e.g., printed words are separated by spaces), and conventions of written English language (e.g., left-to-right, top-to-bottom sequence) (Strickland & Schickedanz, 2004); how books work (Duke, Bennett–Armistead & Moses, 2005).

Echo and choral reading activity to reinforce fluency in which the teacher reads a line or passage and the children echo it back

Emerging/emergent literacy stages children go through to reach conventional literacy

English language learners those whose primary spoken language is not English

Fluency involves accurate decoding, automatic word recognition; the appropriate use of stress, pitch, and suitable phrasing, or the prosodic elements of language (Morrow, Gambrell, & Pressley, 2003)

Genres categories of books, including narrative, informational, wordless, predictable, procedural, poetry (Duke & Bennett–Armistead, 2003)

Graphemes written alphabet symbols

Invented spelling temporary forms of phonetic spelling that children use while on their way to conventional spelling

Letter–sound association ability to connect a letter name to the sound made by the symbol

Movable letters sets of alphabet letters that can be manipulated to form words

Onsets and rimes beginning consonant (the onset) in a word, followed an ending chunk constituted by a vowel and any consonants that follow (e.g., tall, ball, wall, fall). Rimes are also referred to as *phonograms* or *word families* and are not the same as a rhyme.

Open-ended question a question posed that draws people out, prompting them to elaborate (e.g., What do you think . . .? How else could we . . .? What's your idea? What would happen if . . .?) as opposed to a closed-ended question that requires only a one-word answer (What shape is this? How are you? Do you know what this is?) (Kostelnik et al., 2006).

Oral language expressive language ability, including breadth of vocabulary

Phonemic awareness understanding that words are made up of a number of sounds or phonemes; ability to blend and segment words; ability to manipulate sounds to form different words

Phonics strategies for teaching children symbol–sound relationships to enhance decoding abilities

Phonological awareness ability to hear differences and similarities in the sounds of words and parts of words. The awareness of individual sounds and groups of sounds in words, including the ability to separate words into syllables or beats; blend sounds into words; segment sounds into words; recognize and generate words with similar beginning, middle, and ending sounds; move sounds around to make new words (Bennett–Armistead et al., 2005, 36)

Portfolio selected collection of children's work samples

Prosody stress, rhythm, pitch, intonation, rate, and phrasing implicit in oral reading to provide appropriate expression

Readers' theater children's performance of a narrative or expository text that has been read together

Rhyme two or more words that end with the same sound

Scaffolded writing strategy to move children forward toward their understanding of writing structures (words, spaces, sentences, punctuation) and toward independent writing

Segmentation breaking words into discrete phonemes

Silent picture walk paging sequentially and silently through a picture book to give children a sense of the text and to engage their interest prior to actual reading

Story retelling asking children to reiterate a story that has been read, describing important elements of the story, and moving from the beginning, to the middle, and to the end

Stretching words the act of stretching words out by slowing pronunciation of each sound to promote phonological awareness

Student-led conferencing having children take the lead in sharing the contents of their portfolios with peers, parents, or other interested persons

Wordless books picture books that do not contain print; books in which meaning is drawn from the pictures

References

Barone, D. M., & L. M. Morrow, eds. (2003). *Literacy and young children.* New York: Guilford Press.

Barr, R., C. Blachowicz, R. Buhle, C. Chaney, C. Ivy, & G. Súarez–Silva. (2002). *Technical manual—Illinois snapshot of early literacy: Field test year 2000–2001.* Springfield: Illinois State Board of Education.

Bennett-Armistead, V. S., N. K. Duke, & A. M. Moses. (2005). *Literacy and the youngest learner.* New York: Scholastic.

Biggar, H. (2005). NAEYC recommendations on screening and assessment of young English-language learners. *Young Children,* 60(6), 44–51.

Blachowicz, C., C. Obrochta, & E. Fogelberg. (2005). Literacy coaching for change, *Educational Leadership,* 62(6), 55–58.

Bodrova, E., & D. J. Leong. (2001). *The tools of the mind project: A case of implementing the Vygotskian approach in America's early childhood and primary classrooms.* Geneva, Switzerland: UNESCO, International Bureau of Education.

Bodrova, E., & D. J. Leong. (2003). Learning and development of preschool children: The Vygotskian perspective. In *Vygotsky's educational theory in cultural context,* ed. A. Kozulin, B. Gindis, V. Agier, & S. Miller, 156–76. New York: Cambridge University Press.

Bodrova, E., & D. J. Leong. (2006). Vygotskian perspectives on teaching and learning early literacy. In *Handbook of early literacy research,* ed. S. B. Neuman & D. K. Dickinson, 243–56. New York: Guilford Press.

Bower, B. (2004). Words in the brain: Reading program spurs neural rewrite in kids. *Science News Online.* Available online, www.science-news.org/articles/20040508/fob/.asp.

Bruer, J. (1999). *The myth of the first three years.* New York: Free Press.

Charlesworth, R., C. H. Hart, D. C. Burts, R. H. Thomasson, J. Mosely, & P. O. Fleege. (1993). Measuring the developmental appropriateness of kindergarten teachers' beliefs and practices. *Early Childhood Research Quarterly,* 8, 255–76.

Cobb, C. (2005). Literacy teams: Sharing leadership to improve student learning. *The Reading Teacher*, 58(5), 472–74.

Cruz, Josue Jr. (2005). Embracing a vocabulary of inclusiveness. *Young Children*, 60(6), 6.

Cummins, J. (1981). The role of primary language development in promoting educational success for language minority students. In *Schooling and language minority students: A theoretical framework*, ed. California State Department of Education, 3–49. Los Angeles: Evaluation, Dissemination and Assessment Center, California State University.

Cunningham, P. (2000). *Phonics they use*. New York: Longman.

Cunningham, P. (2005). If they don't read much, how they ever gonna get good? *The Reading Teacher*, 59(1), 88–90.

David, J., ed. (2005). English language learners. Head Start Bulletin, Issue No. 78, p. 40. *Head Start Bulletin*. Washington, DC: U.S. Department of Health and Human Services.

Davis, D. (2000). *Supporting parent, family, and community involvement in your school*. Portland, OR: Northwest Regional Educational Laboratory.

Dickinson, D. K., A. McCabe, & M. J. Essex. (2006). A window of opportunity we must open to all: The case for preschools with high-quality support for language and literacy. In *Handbook of early literacy research, vol. 2*, ed. D. K. Dickinson and S. B. Neuman, 11–28. New York: Guilford Press.

Dickinson, D. K., A. McCabe, & K. Sprague. (2003). Teacher rating of oral language and literacy (TROLL): Standards-based rating tool. *The Reading Teacher*, 56(6), 554–65.

Diller, D. (2003). *Literacy work stations: Making centers work*. Portland, ME: Stenhouse.

Duke, N. K., & V. S. Bennett-Armistead. (2003). *Reading and writing informational text in the primary grades: Research-based practices*. New York: Scholastic.

Duke, N. K., V. S. Bennett-Armistead, & A. M. Moses. (2005). *Literacy and the youngest learner*. New York: Scholastic.

Dunn, L., & S. Kontos. (1997). What have we learned about developmentally appropriate practice? *Young Children*, 52(5), 4–13.

Ehri, L. C., & T. Roberts. (2006). The roots of learning to read and write: Acquisition of letters and phonemic awareness. In *Handbook of early literacy research*, ed. S. B. Neuman & D. K. Dickinson, 113–31. New York: Guilford Press.

Epstein, J. (2001). *School, family, and community partnerships*. Boulder, CO: Westview Press.

Epstein, J., K. C. Salinas, B. Simon, L. Costas, M. Sanders, N. Jansora, & F. Van Vores. (2002). *School, family & community partnerships: Your handbook for action*. Thousand Oaks, CA: Sage.

Ericsson, K. A. (2002). Attaining excellence through deliberate practice: Insights from the study of expert performance. In *The pursuit of excellence in education*, ed. M. Ferrari. Hillsdale, NJ: Erlbaum.

Finney, S. (2003). *Independent activities that keep kids learning . . . while you teach small groups*. New York: Scholastic.

Fox, M. (1997). Personal theory of whole language: A teacher–researcher–writer reflects. *The Australian Journal of Language and Literacy*, 20, 122–29.

Fullan, M. (2002). The change leader. *Educational Leadership*, 59(8), 16–20.

Gallagher, K. C. (2005). Brain research and early childhood development: A primer for developmentally appropriate practice. *Young Children*, 60(4), 12–20.

Gardner, H. (1993). *Multiple intelligences: The theory in practice*. New York: Basic.

Gee, J. P. (2001). A sociocultural perspective on early literacy development. In *Handbook of early literacy research*, ed. S. B. Neuman & D. K. Dickinson, 30–40. New York: Guilford Press.

Glasser, W. (1998). *Choice theory in the classroom*. New York: Harper Perennial.

Goldenberg, C. (2001). Making schools work for low-income families in the 21st century. In *Handbook of early literacy research*, ed. S. B. Neuman & D. K. Dickinson, 211–31. New York: Guilford Press.

Graves, M. F., & J. Fitzgerald. (2003). Scaffolding reading experiences for multilingual classrooms. In *English learners*, ed. G. G. Garcia, 96–124. Newark, DE: International Reading Association.

Gunning, T. (2000). *Building words: A resource manual for teaching word analysis and spelling strategies*. Englewood Cliffs, NJ: Prentice Hall.

Gunning, T. G. (2002). *Building literacy in the content areas*. Englewood Cliffs, NJ: Prentice Hall.

Gurian, M., & K. Stevens. (2005). *The minds of boys*. San Francisco: Jossey-Bass.

Halliday, M. A. K. (1975). *Learning how to mean: Exploration in the development of language.* London: Edward Arnold.

Harms, T., R. M. Clifford, & D. Cryer. (1998). *Early childhood environment rating scale—revised edition.* New York: Teachers College Press.

Harris, A. J., & E. R. Sipay. (1990). *How to increase reading ability.* 9th ed. New York: Longman.

Hart, C. H., D. C. Burts, & R. Charlesworth. (1997). Integrated developmentally appropriate practice: From theory to practice. In *Integrated developmentally appropriate curriculum and developmentally appropriate practice, birth to age 8,* ed. C. H. Hart, D. C. Burts, & R. Charlesworth, 1–27. Albany: State of New York Press.

Hart, C. H., D. C. Burts, M. A. Durland, R. Charlesworth, M. DeWolf, & P. O. Fleege. (1998). Stress behaviors and activity type participation of preschoolers in more or less developmentally appropriate classrooms: SES and sex differences. *Journal of Research in Childhood Education*, 12(2), 176–96.

Hart, B., & T. Risley. (2003). The early catastrophe: The 30 million word gap by age. *American Educator*, 4–9.

Hemmeter, M. L., K. L. Maxwell, J. J. Ault, & J. W. Schuster. (2001). *Assessment of practices in early elementary classrooms (APEEC).* New York: Teachers College Press.

Henderson, A. T., & K. L. Mapp. (2002). *A new wave of evidence: Annual synthesis 2002.* Southwest Educational Development Laboratory: National Center for Connections with Family & Community Schools. www.sedl.org.

Herbert, E. (2001). *The power of portfolios: What children can teach us about learning and assessment.* San Francisco: Jossey-Bass.

Hernández, A. (2003). Making content instruction accessible for English language learners. In *English learners*, ed. G. G. Garcia, 125–51. Newark, DE: International Reading Association.

Hernandez, H. (1989). *Multicultural education: A teacher's guide to content and process.* Columbus, OH: Merrill.

Huttenlocher, P. R. (2002). *Neural plasticity: The effects of environment on the development of the cerebral cortex.* Cambridge, MA: Harvard University Press.

Invernizzi, M., F. Johnson, D. R. Bear, & S. R. Templeton. (2003). *Words their way: Word sorts within word pattern spellers.* Englewood Cliffs, NJ: Prentice Hall.

Jensen, E. (1998). *Teaching with the brain in mind.* Alexandria, VA: Association for Supervision and Curriculum Development.

Johnson, L., & J. Mermin. (1994). Easing children's entry to school: Home visits help. *Young Children*, 49(5), 62–68.

Kohn, A. (2004). *What does it mean to be well educated?* Boston: Beacon Press.

Koplow, L. (1996). *Unsmiling faces: How preschools can heal.* New York: Teachers College Press.

Kostelnik, M. J., A. K. Soderman, & A. P. Whiren. (2007). *Developmentally appropriate curriculum: Best practices in early childhood education.* 4th ed. Upper Saddle River, NJ: Prentice Hall.

Kostelnik, M. J., A. P. Whiren, A. K. Soderman, & K. S. Gregory. (2006). *Guiding chidren's social development.* 5th ed. New York: Thompson Delmar Learning.

LaFreniere, P. J., & J. E. Dumas. (1995). *Social competence and behavior evaluation (SCBE), preschool edition.* Los Angeles, CA: Western Psychological Services.

Laturnau, J. (2003). Standards-based instruction for English language learners. In *English learners*, ed. G. G. Garcia, 286–307. Newark, DE: International Reading Association.

LeBuffe, P. A., & J. A. Naglieri. (1998). *Devereux Early Childhood Assessment* (DECA). Lewisville, NC: Kaplan Press.

Lenters, K. (2004). No half measures: Reading instruction for young second-language learners. *The Reading Teacher*, 58(4), 328–36.

Little-Soldier, L. (1992). Working with Native American children. *Young Children*, 47(6), 15–21.

Lopez, E. J., L. Salas, & J. P. Flores. (2005). Hispanic preschool children. What about assessment and intervention? *Young Children*, 60(6), 48–59.

McDonald, N. L., & D. Fisher. (2006). *Teaching literacy through the arts.* New York: Guilford Press.

McTighe, J., & K. O'Connor. (November 2005). Seven practices for effective learning, *Educational Leadership*, 63(3), 10–17.

Mendoza, J., L. Katz, A. S. Robertson, & D. Rothenberg. (2003). Connecting with schools in the early years. *Clearinghouse on Early Education and Parenting (CEEP)*. Urbana-Champaign: University of Illinois.

Millard, E. (2003). Towards a literacy of fusion: New times, new teaching, new learning? *Literacy*, 37(1), 3.

Miller, D. F. (2004). *Positive child guidance.* Albany, NY: Delmar.

Moore, P. A., & A. Lyon. (2005). *Teaching young readers.* New York: Scholastic.

Morrow, L. M., L. B. Gambrell, & M. Pressley, eds. (2003). *Best practices in literacy instruction.* 2nd ed. New York: Guilford Press.

Nagel, K. B. (2001). *Our silly garden.* New York: Scholastic.

Nathan, R. (1995). Parents, projects, and portfolios: 'Round and about community building in room 14. *Language Arts*, 72, 82–87.

National Center for Educational Statistics (NCES). (1998). *Education attitudes and behavior.* Washington, DC: U.S. Department of Education.

National Parent Teacher Association (PTA). (2004). *National standards for parent/family involvement programs.* Author.

Nations, S., & Alonso, M. (2001). *Primary literacy centers: Making reading and writing STICK!* Gainsville, FL: Maupin House.

Neuman, S. B. (2006). The knowledge gap: Implications for early education. In *Handbook of early literacy research*, vol. 2., ed. D. K. Dickinson and S. B. Neuman, 29–40. New York: Guilford Press.

Opitz, M. F., & M. P. Ford. (2004). What do I do with the rest of the kids? Ideas for meaningful independent activities during small-group reading instruction. *The Reading Teacher,* 58(4), 394–96.

Paley, V. G. (1984). *Boys and girls: Superheroes in the doll corner.* Chicago: University of Chicago Press.

Restak, R. (2003). *The new brain.* New York: Rodale.

Routman, R. (2000). *Conversations.* Portsmouth, NH: Heinemann.

Rubin, R., & V. G. Carlan. (May 2005). Using writing to understand bilingual children's literacy development. *The Reading Teacher*, 58(8), 728–39.

Salinger, T. (2006). Policy decisions in early childhood assessment. In *Handbook of early literacy research, vol. 2*, ed. D. K. Dickinson and S. B. Neuman, 427–44. New York: Guilford Press.

Scharer, P. L., G. S. Pinnell, C. Lyons, & I. Fountas. (2005). Becoming an engaged reader. *Educational Leadership*, 63(2), 24–29.

Schickedanz, J. A. (2003). Engaging preschoolers in code learning. Some thoughts about preschool teachers' concerns. In *Literacy and young chil-*

dren, ed. D. M. Barone and L. M. Morrow, 121–39. New York: Guilford Press.

Seefeldt, C. (2005). *How to work with standards in the early childhood classroom.* New York: Teachers College Press.

Shaywitz, S. (2003). *Overcoming dyslexia: A new and complete science-based program for reading problems at any level.* New York: Alfred A. Knopf.

Shonkoff, D., & J. P. Phillips. (2000). *From neurons to neighborhoods: The science of early childhood development.* Washington, DC: National Academy Press.

Smith, M. W., & D. K. Dickinson. (2002). *Early language and literacy classroom observation (ELLCO).* New York: Brookes Publishing.

Smyth, G. (2003). *Helping bilingual children to access the curriculum.* London: David Fulton Publishers.

Soderman, A. K. (September 2005). *Enhancing the school readiness of high-poverty children.* Presented at the 15th Annual Conference on Quality in Early Childhood Education. European Early Childhood Education Research Association (EECERA), Dublin, Ireland.

Soderman, A. K., & L. Adams. (August 2005). *Children's and teachers' narratives about emerging literacy.* Presented at the European Early Childhood Education and Research Association (EECERA), Lefkosia, Cyprus.

Soderman, A. K., S. Chikkara, C. Hsiu-Ching, & E. Kuo. (1999). Gender differences that affect emerging literacy in first grade children: The U.S., India and Taiwan. *International Journal of Early Childhood,* 31(2), 9–16.

Soderman, A. K., K. S. Gregory, & L. T. McCarty. (2005). *Scaffolding emergent literacy: A child-centered approach for preschool through grade 5.* 2nd ed. Boston: Allyn & Bacon.

Strickland, D. S. & J. A. Schickedanz. (2004). *Learning about print in preschool.* Newark, DE: International Reading Association.

Tabors, P. (1997). *One child, two languages.* New York: Paul H. Brooks.

Teale, W. H. (2003). Questions about early literacy learning and teaching that need asking—and some that don't. In *Literacy and young children: Research-based practices,* ed. D. M. Barone and L. M. Marrow, 23–44. New York: Guilford Press.

Farrell, P. (2000). *The early years are learning years.* Report from the Ready to Succeed Blue Ribbon Committee, September. East Lansing, MI: Michigan State University.

Thelen, P., & A. K. Soderman. (2002). *Running a successful kindergarten orientation: A round-up guide for elementary principals and teachers.* Lansing, MI: Lansing School District Safe Schools/Healthy Students Initiative.

U.S. Department of Education. (1997). *Fathers' involvement in their children's schools.* Washington, DC: U.S. Department of Education, Office of Educational Research and Improvement.

U.S. Department of Education, National Center for Education Statistics. (2006). *America's children: Key national indicators of well-being.* National Household Education Surveys Program. Washington, DC: Author.

VanderZanden, J. W. (2003). *Human development.* Boston: McGraw Hill.

Volk, D., & S. Long. (2005). Challenging myths of the deficit perspective: Honoring children's literacy resources, *Young Children*, 60(6), 12–19.

Watson, M. (2003). Attachment theory and challenging behaviors: Reconstructing the nature of relationships. *Young Children*, 58(4), 12–20.

Whitehurst, G. J., & C. J. Lonigan. (2001). Emergent literacy: Development from prereaders to readers. In *Handbook of early literacy research*, ed. S. B. Neuman and D. K. Dickinson, 11–29. New York: Guilford Press.

Wingert, P., & B. Kantrowitz. (1997). Why Andy couldn't read. *Newsweek*, 103(17), 56–64.

Winograd, P., L. Flores-Duenas, & H. Arrington. (2003). Best practices in literacy assessment. In *Best practices in literacy instruction,* 2nd ed., ed. L. M. Morrow, L. B. Gambrell, and M. Pressley, 210–44. New York: Guilford Press.

Winzer, M., & K. Mazurek. (1998). *Special education in multicultural contexts.* Upper Saddle River, NJ: Merrill Prentice Hall.

Index